THE CITIZEN

ROY FISHER (1958)

Roy Fisher

THE CITIZEN
and the making of *City*

EDITED BY
PETER ROBINSON

BLOODAXE BOOKS

ISBN: 978 1 78037 596 0

First published 2022 by
Bloodaxe Books Ltd,
Eastburn,
South Park,
Hexham,
Northumberland NE46 1BS

www.bloodaxebooks.com
For further information about Bloodaxe titles
please visit our website and join our mailing list
or write to the above address for a catalogue.

Supported using public funding by
**ARTS COUNCIL
ENGLAND**

Cover design: Neil Astley & Pamela Robertson-Pearce.

Printed in Great Britain by Bell & Bain Limited, Glasgow, Scotland, on
acid-free paper sourced from mills with FSC chain of custody certification.

CONTENTS

NOTE ON TEXTS

The following list offers an outline sequence for texts included here, as well as ones not included relating to *City*'s composition:

a. *The Citizen*
A hand-written prose text of 103 pages, some partially mutilated, in a blue hard-bound, unlined notebook, dated at the front *November 1959*. This is published in full below.

b. A *Citizen* notebook
A post-composition outline of the contents of *The Citizen*, the individual sections numbered to 117 and identified by names or short descriptions, though there are no more than numbers for sections 74 to 117. This is followed by two journal entries dated 10 and 11 November 1960. The journal entries are published below.

c. Poems included in the various versions of *City*
These are 'A Lullaby and Exhortation for the Unwilling Hero', 'The Entertainment of War', 'North Area', 'By the Pond', 'The Sun Hacks, 'Toyland', 'The Judgment', 'The Hill Behind the Town', 'The Poplars', 'Starting to Make a Tree', 'The Wind at Night', 'Do Not Remain Too Much Alone' (including an 11-line coda by Michael Shayer), 'Night Walkers', and 'The Park'. For details of their first publications, see the extracts from 'Roy Fisher: A Bibliography' by Derek Slade included in the Notes below.

d. Related poems not used in any versions of *City*
These are 'Midlanders', written on 12 January 1957 which first appeared in *Mica* (Fall 1961) and 'Lost, Now', written

on 30 December 1960 and which appeared in *Poetry and Audience* c. 1961. 'The Fog at Birmingham', 'Sea Monster in Hospital Shed', and 'Where We Are' are not previously published and so not readily dateable, though all in existence before mid-1960, when referred to in correspondence. They are published here. Other related poems ('Script City', 'Something Unmade', 'Results', 'Last Brief Maxims', 'After Midnight', 'Variations (on Bag's Groove)', 'The Bachelors Stripped Bare by their Bride', and 'Division of Labour' can be found in *Slakki: New & Neglected Poems* (Hexham: Bloodaxe Books, 2016), pp. 39-43, 48-51 and 56.

e. *City* (Worcester: Migrant Press, 1961)

A stapled, printed pamphlet of 21 text pages including the 'Preface' by Michael Shayer. This is reprinted below.

f. *Then Hallucination: City II* (Worcester: Migrant Press, 1962)

A stapled, duplicated pamphlet of 9 pages containing further prose sections extracted from *The Citizen* and first published in *Kulchur* (New York) 2:6, Summer 1962. It is reprinted below. Two numbered, surviving sections, once other passages had been excerpted for the revised *City*, were included in *The Cut Pages* (London: Fulcrum Press, 1971) under the title 'Hallucinations' and have since appeared thus in collected editions of Fisher's work.

g. CITY: Roy Fisher typescript (*c.* 1962-63)

A large unpublished typescript of 24 pages, constituting an intermediate version that foreshadows the definitive text in its choice of poems and prose sections. It also includes the paragraphs that had made up *Then Hallucinations* and the two poems, 'Night Walkers' and 'The Judgment', these items subsequently excluded. It is dated on internal and contextual evidence as *c.* 1962-63 and survives because a carbon copy was posted to Gael Turnbull. It is published below.

h. *City* in *Living Arts* 1 (1963)

This text is close to the definitive version, though 'The Judgment' and 'Night Walkers' are still included, and there are a number of local variants in punctuation, largely the suppression of semi-colons in favour of full stops, and some small revisions in the prose paragraphs. This is not printed here. The excluded poems are available in item g.

i. *City* in *Collected Poems 1968* (London: Fulcrum Press, 1969)

The definitive text of *City* subsequently reprinted in the two volumes of *Poems* from Oxford University Press (1980 and 1987) as well as the Bloodaxe Books editions of *The Dow Low Drop: New & Selected Poems* (1996) and *The Long and the Short of It* (2005 and 2012). Some slight variants have crept into this text with its reprintings. Published below is the Fulcrum text.

This gathering of materials is not the first posthumous publication of work by Roy Fisher. The Flood Editions re-presentation of *A Furnace* (2018) appeared after the poet's death but had been authorised and discussed before 21 March 2017. Fisher did not authorise, and might not have authorised in his lifetime, the printing and reprinting of this book's materials. Though unaware that *The Citizen* had survived, or, for that matter, of the extent of Fisher's literary estate, I did discuss the idea of a *City* variorum with him while working on *Slakki: New & Neglected Poems* (2016). He didn't encourage me; but nor did he exactly rule out such a volume. 'The words of a dead man / Are modified in the guts of the living,' wrote W.H. Auden of Yeats's death, and though it is incumbent upon an editor not to modify the poet's words, I am aware of differently inflecting some of his oeuvre by making these writings available now.

Reading this chronological arrangement of the texts from cover to cover will involve various experiences of *déjà vu*, for some passages, such as the opening two prose paragraphs, carry through from *The Citizen* to the 1969 version of *City*. Other poems and passages of prose appear more than once, while a large part of *The Citizen* and other prose passages, such the final sections of the 1961 *City* and *Then Hallucinations*, make only the one appearance. The book can be read in reverse order, tracking back from Fisher's definitive version through the work's intermediate stages to its sources in the separate poetry and prose. Fisher's recording of the definitive text has been made available with this publication on the Bloodaxe website. It derives from the 1977 Nimbus recording made for an LP called *City: Poetry and Prose by Roy Fisher read by the Author* (Amber 7102).

The Citizen, the workbook comments, the related poems, *Then Hallucinations*, the two variants of *City* and the definitive text have been supplemented here by a selection from Fisher's published comments on the work, excerpted by Derek Slade from interviews and occasional prose works, and a secondary bibliography of critical writings. The notes appended indicate the dates of composition and publication for the individual poems that were inserted between the prose passages in the versions of this work. These derive in their entirety from Derek Slade's bibliography. Sources are provided for the anthologised comments from Fisher's interviews and other ancillary prose. The text of *The Citizen* reproduces as nearly as possible Roy Fisher's surviving manuscript. A few misspellings have been corrected, and the presentation of direct speech has been standardised, as have a few hyphenations of compound adjectives.

For their various contributions to the assembling and editing of this book, my thanks go to Simon Collings, who transcribed *The Citizen* from Fisher's manuscript notebook, to Derek Slade who made his bibliographical knowledge available once again and edited Fisher's comments on his work, to Adam Piette and Peter Makin whose conversation helped focus the issues involved in presenting this material, to Amanda Bernstein for her conversation, enthusiasm, and work on the Fisher archive that pointed me to the large typescript, to Michael Shayer for his memories of work on the Migrant Press publication, his providing a rare copy of the original *Then Hallucinations* for use during this work, and permission to publish extracts from his correspondence, to Jill Turnbull for permission to quote from Gael Turnbull's correspondence, and to Sukey Fisher for advice and permission from the Estate of Roy Fisher to publish. Lastly, my thanks go to Neil Astley and the team at Bloodaxe Books for their commitment to this project and their various expertise in helping to bring it to fruition.

INTRODUCTION

1. Circumstances and Materials

On Tuesday 4 February 1958, *The Birmingham Mail* published a 'Jazz Panorama' by Fred Norris which profiled the twenty-seven-year-old Roy Fisher, describing him as a 'man who teaches drama by day, plays jazz piano by night, and writes self-styled "off-beat" poetry in whatever spare time he has left'. 'Roy,' he reports, 'who lives at 224, The Broadway, Walsall, has only recently returned to the Midland jazz scene. For the last four years he has been teaching in Devon.' This article includes a brief statement of aesthetic allegiances that sees the spare-time writer primed for what would happen over the next few years:

> I have been told my poetry is 'off-beat' and that is how I regard it. I do not write in traditional metres. I write in free verse. Jazz is a robust music. It is creative. It is worthless trying to play jazz if you have nothing to say. The same applies to poetry. I write about the things I see, the way I see them – cities, modern life, people and their thoughts.

Returning with his wife, Barbara Venables, from Newton Abbot to his native Birmingham, Fisher had taken up a post in a teacher training college. Working by day in education and then, as later detailed in his prose memoir 'License my Roving Hands', travelling distances across the city at unusual hours to and from jazz-club gigs, Fisher was reacquainting himself with the place of his birth at a time of great change. From such life experiences, returned to in the 'Introit: 12 November 1958' to *A Furnace*

(1986), emerged the two key elements – a number of independently conceived poems, and a hybrid prose text – which would go towards the collaged materials of *City*, an assemblage that, substantially revised, would come to be appreciated as both a decisive poetic response to this mid-century British experience of urban demolition and renewal, and also its poet's signature work.

In a letter to his friend and fellow-poet Gael Turnbull, then based in Ventura, California, probably written during 1960, Fisher reported on recent productivity:

> I have started writing like mad: an odd feeling. After so much idleness I'm sweating over four projects: – making a collection of fairly solid poems; writing a long sequence of poems on a theme; a square carnivorous novel (just begun); and a sententious prose book, about the length of a short novel, called *the Citizen*. This is about a quarter done; a *mélange* of evocation, maundering, imagining, fiction and autobiography. I'm doing all this so as to be able to have a look at myself & see what I think. (I did say 'like mad.'!) The evidence assembled so far is, after all, rather scanty.

The Citizen is revealed to be a work in which Fisher did give himself permission to 'have a look at myself & see what I think' – what he thought manifested in various strata of self-analytical marginalia. In doing so, he found both his core materials, and a range of modes for addressing them, since *The Citizen* contains more or less documentary accounts of alterations being wrought to Birmingham at the time, observations fed by memories of his childhood and family, a comparing and contrasting of the old city and the new one, all of these placed alongside more feverishly narrative, sexually troubled, and hallucinatory sections. There are further passages which suggest the piece was projected as a form of *nouveau roman* with a combination of remembered and imaginary characters, to which the mysterious first-person narrator (the eponymous citizen, presumably) can variously relate, along with indications of some minimal plotting and narrative. It contains some of Fisher's most vivid writing.

The story of how this 'sententious prose book' became the ur-text for a hybrid collage of poetry and prose, which would eventually be seen as Fisher's self-defining perform-ance, has complexities of its own, ones that items in the poet's archive, now at the University of Sheffield, have made it possible for the first time to disentangle. It had been fairly widely known, since Donald Davie drew attention to it in his chapter devoted to Fisher in *Thomas Hardy and British Poetry* (1973), that *City* existed in two versions, a pamphlet published by Migrant Press in 1961, and the distinctly variant text with some different poems and prose passages which formed the entitled second section to the Fulcrum Press *Collected Poems 1968*.

Fisher's death on 21 March 2017 and the discovery of his archive's contents added to the picture in a number of ways. The most prominent of these was the discovery that *The Citizen* had indeed survived. Dated 'November 1959', though with some pages cut out and others partly excised, its text is preserved in a blue hardback notebook (also containing two later prose experiments, *Peter Cooper* and *Album of Year 62*, which were written in mid-1964). Further survivals included notes and attempts to shape and extend the prose text in an unlined 'City of Birmingham Education Committee' school exercise book with a pale grey-green soft cover, and the word *Citizen* inscribed on it.

This notebook appears to have been employed at the time the manuscript of *The Citizen* was heavily marked up, annotated, and partially mutilated. The entries consist in twelve pages of various numbered lists with named parts, and many unnamed (and unwritten) ones reaching as far as no. 117. The opening section, for example, which appears in both *The Citizen* and *City*, is called 'Demolished houses at Hockley Hill'. These lists are also heavily annotated with, for instance, red biro underlines marking sections that were used as the prose paragraphs in *City*. The lists are followed by four and a half pages of notes-to-self, dated the 10 and 11 November 1960, which have been published below as an authorial afterword to what survives of *The Citizen*.

Fisher's archive contains an undated carbon copy of 'CITY by Roy Fisher', a text that includes almost all of the additional prose passages called *Then Hallucinations*, described in handwriting on their surviving typescript as a supplement to *City*, and first published by Migrant Press in 1962. They would find their definitive form as 'Hallucinations' in *The Cut Pages* (1971). The archive also includes, intriguingly, the Contents page for a putative collection of poems called *Starting to Make a Tree* that was submitted to the Hutchinson publishing company on 2 October 1961 and, presumably, rejected.

Its significance lies in the fact that the projected collection of individual poems was assembled and submitted after the publication of the Migrant pamphlet *City*, which came out in June of that year (though dated May in the text). The proposed collection contains, as the title poem indicates, pieces already used in that published volume, now being presented in this putative first collection as stand-alone poems. The book would have contained pieces that are to be found in *City*, others now in the *Early Poems* section of *Collected Poems 1968*, some poems that only found print in *Slakki: New & Neglected Poems* (2016), and others that remain unpublished.

These materials are supplemented by the evidence in correspondence between Turnbull and Fisher held at the former's archive at the Scottish Poetry Library in Edinburgh, and letters sent by Shayer to Fisher after the Migrant *City* had been published (the poet's to Shayer have not survived). They are informed by telephone conversations I had with the poet while assembling *Slakki* during 2015 and 2016. In the light, too, of his own published comments on *City* assembled for this volume by Derek Slade, I offer an account of how the collage found its final form and came to have the prominence in the poet's oeuvre that it does.

2. The Compositional Process

On 16 August 1961, after the appearance of the Migrant *City*, Turnbull sent Fisher his response to its publication:

> My only real disappointment with it is that it isn't *LONGER* – I feel very persistently that it needs more extent, a greater bulk of material – that it (especially the prose) isn't something to be pared down to a concise focus, but should be allowed to spread out – and I wonder how *much* more material you have – and, further, wonder if it would be possible to add a supplement to it? another six or eight pages?

Turnbull's proposal was to prompt the construction of

Then Hallucinations, from which came materials that facilitated the eventual enlargement of the prose passages in the later sections of the revised version of *City*. A draft typescript of *Then Hallucinations* with authorial corrections in ink on this text, also mined from *The Citizen*, has survived in the poet's archive.

Responding to Turnbull's letter, Fisher reports further on the impetus and development of his 'sententious prose book':

> As to the size, shape and all, of it – that's an odd story. What happened was that about 18 months ago, I decided that the only way I could say anything sensible was to write a series of prose poems or intensified reports about what I was seeing and how I saw it. A thing of the *cahier* sort. I got a notebook and started building these things up – all in prose. When I saw I was putting a great deal of my consciousness across in a way in which I hadn't seen it before, I got carried away and started to plan all sorts of themes and near-story elements, which I wasn't ready for (because the book was not CITY but CITIZEN and really a sort of exploration of Dedalus and Bloom rolled into one; and this examination of myself was a useful private task but not a communicative thing).

The poet's getting carried away perhaps explains the lists of episodes, some of them without any description of contents, in the *Citizen* workbook, and their petering out presumably prompted those postscript-like reflections. Writing to Turnbull, Fisher describes attempting to respond to the call from Shayer, in his role at Migrant Press, to produce a work for their list:

> So I could then get on and write the CITY poems, about a dozen, some of which you may not have seen. Have you seen these: WHERE WE ARE; SEA-MONSTER; or

HOSPITAL SHED; LOST NOW; DIVISION OF LABOUR; THE PARK? If not, I'll let you have them. Well – those got somewhere – some of them, but by January [1961] I was feeling pretty played out, largely from other reasons. When Michael asked for a pamphlet I wanted to sit down and write something new and compact; but it didn't come. I put together a draft consisting of most of the relevant poems and some of the great quantity of prose I had; on second glance this seemed rather doughy and safe – flat-bottomed, with all the points made twice. (Secretly I think it might have been more popular that way!) I was so disgusted with the discovery of how cautious I'd been, covering my tracks etc., that I let Michael sort the stuff out and print what he wanted.

Of the fourteen different poems included in the various versions of *City* only 'The Park' is listed in Fisher's letter, at a point when it did not yet form the collage's definitive coda.

'SEA-MONSTER; or HOSPITAL SHED' turns out to be a single poem, also existing in a typescript called 'Sea Monster in Hospital Shed', which I have included below among the small group of related unpublished poems. In a 14 June 1961 letter, Shayer notes: 'I still think Fog at Birmingham (which I am keeping) has a power of its own. I am also keeping The Bachelors stripped bare; Sea Monster; Something unmade; Variations on Bags Groove; and Midlanders.' All the other poetry referred to above in the letters to Turnbull or from Shayer can be found either in the versions of *City* itself, or in the second and third sections of *Slakki: New & Neglected Poems*. The relevance of Marcel Duchamp as an inspiration and guide is underlined in the final two paragraphs of *Then Hallucinations*, a passage which does not derive from *The Citizen* as it has survived.

A typed letter from Shayer, dated in Fisher's hand 'c.14.ii.61', gives a sense of that crucial moment in *City*'s evolution. Shayer has 'managed one reading of your manuscript' and observes that the 'prose is one with the quality that had already drawn me in some of your Birmingham poems. *This* is what *I* was after in suggesting the pamphlet.' He adds:

> Look, I think your [*sic*] using your sense of pace, shift of mood, coherence, to choose those poems which can be interleaved and counterpointed with the prose sections. Thinking in terms of a whole that moves and yet completes itself like a musical-....? I'll make suggestions in a few days, if you like. And, alright, maybe I am asking too much, but I'm sure *something* would be achieved by the attempt. You know, the poems would come in, in the way a song comes in, in a musical.

Shayer's report on his attempt to assemble another version is dated in his hand 13 March 1961. He begins: 'here is my first instinctive stumbling towards a pattern in the material you have sent me already', writing that he can 'hear a definite counterpoint of prose and poetry, say: Beginning with your page of prose' and then reports that 'I have all the sheets spread out on the floor':

> as I look through the [*sic*], trying to order and that, wondering about the mixture of poetry and prose, etc. so the memory comes back of Connolly's Unquiet Grave, which is one of the few books I have read many times more than once, and go on so doing. The feeling intensifies that an instrument of expression is here exercising itself indiscriminately as a child with different paints and crayons and pencils, until such time as some myth, some distant point of focus, comes and gathers these things together incredibly more taut in a common focus. If ever I have seen material which merited the

description experimental prose and experimental poetry, it is this. I suspect that nothing further than a rather formal pattern can be drawn, but that this is worth doing both for you and for others that could make use of your experimenting. For what it is worth, my sense is that your medium is prose – at least, your medium for writing about City is prose.

His report on working with Fisher's various texts then turns into a covering letter for the mailing to the poet of what would become the 1961 version of *City*:

> Anyway, purely for an indication of what *I* have felt in your work, here are a selection of your prose and poetry, put in the order and amount, more or less, that I would put it if you died tomorrow, and I was to go ahead and do something with just what I have. I suppose what I do is to allow the prose to introduce the 'place', followed by some poetry doing likewise, but somewhat with different images. Then I let some more prose introduce the people of this place, and some poetry of people too. Then a little political passage and fragmentary but rather more concrete images follow, with a 'personal' statement in prose and a like one (including the bit added in pen) to finish off. This I say deliberately, but in fact I just put them in the order I 'felt' and reasoned out what I had done afterwards.

Shayer concludes by asking: 'Now, is this what kind of structure *you* felt – or very different?'

Fisher's post-publication feelings about what this process produced were subsequently conveyed to Turnbull, when he noted that Shayer has 'presented me in the last section of CITY. This needed doing, and I wouldn't have done it myself. I mean, it needed doing to me, personally; I think it rather distorts what I was trying to do with the urban material.' The first independent publication of his work and the experience of seeing the texts in print had proved painful: 'This business of timidity gave me an upsetting time over the publication of CITY: first of all failing to put it together boldly and then suffering the exposure of it'.

The poet concludes by signing up to Turnbull's enlargement proposal, though we can detect here that he is simultaneously imagining a version that includes further prose passages:

> Yes, I'd like to do some sort of pendant to CITY. I might want it to be more conscious and directed than what you were thinking of. Michael has some stuff he is sending back and I'll let you see some. But I'd really like to write a short descriptive tract. (I'm not critical of Michael's editing of me – I shall be a long time grateful to him for forcing me through the hoop).

In a letter dated 14 June 1961, Shayer had first said that he was returning 'your various elements to you' and also sending '23 more copies of *City*' for personal use. However, he adds 'on second thoughts, I will keep this folder of returnables and 20 Cities (unless you are in a hurry for either) until we next meet (why don't you come down here at a weekend again) and will send you 3 Cities now.' In the same letter he notes that 'looking back on it I eliminated good poems like The Hospital because they were good and could stand on their own two legs, and did not need the supporting context of the rest'. This must refer to 'The Hospital in Winter', because 'Sea Monster in Hospital Shed' is referred to separately in the same letter.

Writing on 11 January 1963, Fisher reports to Turnbull that John Bodley has approached him and asked for a reprint of *City* in *Living Arts* No. 1. He notes: 'In the process, incidentally, I've rehashed the text yet again, for keeps this time: knocked out some bits I don't want, and run the two parts together'. I take this reference to rehashing 'the text yet again' as evidence that the longest typescript, 'CITY by Roy Fisher' is an intermediate state, made after the further excerpting of passages from *The Citizen* that produced *Then Hallucinations* – because it also includes almost all of those prose pieces.

Recasting it for 'CITY by Roy Fisher' constitutes, then, the poet's most sustained effort to convert the Migrant *City* into something that he could, as it were, call his own. There are a number of major revisions: 'Toyland' and 'Do Not Remain Too Much Alone' are removed, though 'The Judgment' and 'Night Walkers' remain for the time being. Then appears 'The Park' in the magazine printed version with its long lines divided in half, and various indentations. There is a great deal more prose added, and the passages of what seem first-personal confession and anxiety that would give the final version its closing distinction have been removed from *Then Hallucinations*, where they first emerged from a further cull of *The Citizen*. The sub-headings in the Migrant text have also all been removed.

This version must have then been used in the winter of 1962-63 to edit for *Living Arts* what became almost the definitive version. For that publication, Fisher shortened the prose by removing the passages from *Then Hallucinations* – ones which would eventually re-emerge as 'Hallucinations'. He retained 'The Judgment' which, with 'Night Walkers', would be removed for the Fulcrum publication, and simplified the lineation of poems such as 'The Park' and 'The Poplars'. An indented typescript of the latter exists on which Fisher has written at the top in pencil: 'Square all lines back to L.H. margins'. This decision postdates the large typescript, which contains the indented version of this and other poems, indicating its temporal location as prior to both the near definitive and definitive publications.

The two parts Fisher refers to in the letter to Turnbull must be, then, what was produced by removing the 'Hallucinations' prose and joining the opening and closing movements together. This, with the future removal of 'The Judgment' and 'Night Walkers' with local editorial revision, would produce the definitive version in the Fulcrum *Collected Poems*. In his prose memoir, 'Debt to Mr Bunting', Fisher allows us a glimpse of that final stage: 'I sat once at a table in Stuart and Deirdre Montgomery's flat overlooking Southampton Row, correcting the galleys of *City* for the Fulcrum Press *Collected Poems 1968*, with Basil sitting quietly in the corner peering at *The Times* with the pages held close to his face. Every time I looked in his direction I felt for an adjective to cut or a construction to contract. It was the nearest I could get to asking for a blessing on my prose.'

3. *City* as Roy Fisher's Signature Work

The poet's reason given in interview and conversation for abandoning *The Citizen* is that he could not get its central character to talk to anyone. As can be seen below, though, other characters do say things in a few of the sections, but when asked by the young Welsh woman 'Don't you talk?' the first-person narrator has no direct speech in reply. The surviving school exercise book provides many further reasons for its abandonment, because, as already noted, the manuscript has not been left in its pristine written form. On different not dateable occasions, Fisher has read over the manuscript adding his pencil comments of a critical kind on paragraphs and sections, crossing out passages, marking others in red biro for extraction, scissoring out pages and tearing out parts of others (none of these various comments are reproduced in the reading text offered below). I asked Michael Shayer if he had seen this notebook and done any of the excising, and he replied that he had not. As implied above, Fisher provided him with the materials, both poems and prose, which he would assemble into the 1961 version. The critical work of evaluation, selection and excision that mark this surviving manuscript remnant of *The Citizen* was, then, Fisher's seeing what he thought.

Deriving from wide reading and individual inspiration were the separate poems that would find their ways into the different versions of *City*. These are the work of a poet who, we should remember, was in his late 20s, experimenting with different modes, from the more documentary styles of 'Toyland' and 'The Entertainment of War' by way of epigrammatic lyrics such as 'By the Pond' and 'The Sun Hacks' (which in one surviving separate typescript is called 'Valley Light'), or the eventually rejected 'The Judgment' and 'Night Walkers', through to the semi-surreal experiments ('Lullaby and Exhortation for the Unwilling Hero' or 'Starting to Make a Tree') and the slightly stiff stanzas with rhymes, repeated lines, and refrains of 'The Hill Behind the Town' or 'The Park'. There are also, it's worth adding, at least two pieces ('The Poplars' and 'Starting to Make a Tree') which skilfully foreshadow the directions that Fisher poetry writing would subsequently take: the lightly built, visually prompted, meditative lyric with laconic observations, and the deadpan surreal prose poem.

Also preserved in the Roy Fisher Archive is the photo-copy of a 5 April 1973 letter to Donald Davie with detailed responses to his gift of *Thomas Hardy and British Poetry*, published that year. This piece of correspondence casts a slightly different light on the relation between the two main published versions of *City* and how they came to be assembled:

> When we put *City* together I made a rather tidy draft. Shayer wanted more 'ruin': I wanted more 'art.' I gave in and let him scatter it: I didn't like the arrangement or the preface then, but I think the preface interesting now.

This is Fisher's response to Davie's use of comments in the Preface describing it as a 'ruined work of art' in his criticism of *City* (on p. 168), while the following is keyed to Davie's criticism of the final poem in the Migrant version (on p. 170):

> Have you really got a text with that 'Mary May' stanza? I don't think I wrote it. But neither do I have a copy of the pamphlet, so far as I know. I certainly never felt that little squib of a poem should stand as an endpiece.

The stanza referred to is in quotation marks in the 1961 *City*, while the 'squib of a poem' refers to his own 'Do Not Remain Too Much Alone', in some typescripts entitled 'I Called It Poetry', to which the 'fade out' in quotation marks was collaged by Shayer. Alluding to, but not naming, *The Citizen*, Fisher adds:

> I depersonalised the prose passages in revision, possibly wrongly. It came from a first draft that was turning into a

narcissistic Durrellesque novel, and I didn't want that to unbalance the tone.

The origins of the prose sections to *City* in a work of a different scale and ambition, composed, it would seem, without thought of communication with readers, may have prompted such anxious revisions, but the comparisons this publication makes possible reveal that in many cases passages are lifted with almost no change directly into the eventually definitive assemblage.

It is important to underline, then, that at *no* point was *City* composed and constructed as a single work. It is very much a collage, and unique among Fisher's writings in being assembled, after composition, from pieces that are to be employed for unplanned tasks and altered by being placed next to one another. What these roles are, and how they came to be so employed, was not a given either, or known in advance, but, as the variant forms of the assemblage indicate, had to be identified by a process of trial and error – which included a measure both of collaboration and friendly disagreement.

Migrant Press had emerged out of Gael Turnbull's biographical and career migrations, and, at the time of the first *City*, was being collaboratively edited by Turnbull and Shayer with Fisher, at one point, running the press's finances, its subscriptions and sales. What appears to have happened is that, at the urging of the other two, Fisher produced his own ur-*City* by excerpting passages from *The Citizen* and interleaving them with some of the poems that were, as Fisher put it, 'lying around'. On the basis of his letter to Davie, it would appear that Shayer judged this version to be over-tidy: 'Shayer wanted more "ruin" while I wanted more "art".' For the purposes of the Migrant pamphlet, his friend was allowed to have his way, and thus the 1961 text, including its Preface and, presumably, the section sub-headings are his work too. Fisher's letter to Davie makes it clear that he does not, in 1973, have a copy of the Migrant edition; and he is not at all sure he even wrote the final refrain section of 'Do Not Remain Too Much Alone', which is perhaps indicatively printed in parentheses. This 'music-hall' ending does not appear in any of the typescripts that survive of this early and never reprinted stand-alone poem. Shayer's correspondence above confirms that it was he who wrote that music-hall-like fade from the stage.

It is clear from subsequent events and documentary evidence that Fisher was made uncomfortable by the shape and publication of Shayer's version, though he would express interest in its Preface twelve years later when writing to Davie. One can see why on both counts. After all, the Migrant *City* was the poet's first stand-alone publication of any kind. In this it inaugurates the beginnings of the place *City* would come to hold in his oeuvre, yet it is prefaced by Shayer's piece of well-meant prose that, even if comparing his writings to those of Joyce, Pound and Eliot, nevertheless declares it 'a ruined work of art'. Fisher thus appears to debut with a publication that is pronounced by no means a shining success. The stakes, anyone might think, were being set far too high, and the writer's failure, his being left with a ruin, might have been thought inevitable. Yet what could have also felt troubling is that this ruin had not exactly been composed – in quite that form at least – by Fisher himself.

The survival of the contents page for *Starting to Make a Tree*, the collection submitted to Hutchinson in October

1961, could indicate just how insignificant, invisible, or provisional a debut Fisher took the Migrant pamphlet to be. Nevertheless, it did have distinguished and influential readers, for the photocopy in my possession derives from J.H. Prynne's (which he has inscribed with his name), Donald Davie possessed a copy in Palo Alto, California, when writing *Thomas Hardy and British Poetry*, as he affirms in his reply to Fisher's letter from the Stanford summer school in France that same April 1973, and the pamphlet was reviewed by Denise Levertov in *Kultur* magazine in the USA. Thus, barely known at the time to its author, his collage was beginning to establish some of its 'signature' credentials.

The next stage of *City*'s emergence as an author-defining work was, according to a Fisher notebook entry from 11 June 2000 and our phone conversations, largely the work of Stuart Montgomery at Fulcrum Press. A collection to have been called *The Ghost of a Paper Bag* – whose earlier existence can still be seen in the mysterious dedication page with those words on it – became *Collected Poems 1968*. This book contains, more strictly described, a radical selection from the poems then existent, which appear as 'Early Poems', including one piece, 'Toyland', which had already been a part of the Migrant *City*, then the stream-lined version of Fisher's redaction of this work, followed by carefully edited versions of two pamphlets, *Interiors with Various Figures* and *The Memorial Fountain*, and concluding in a number of 'Other Poems' written before his writing 'block', which started to descend in 1966 and did not fully let up until 1970.

It is this organisation of the Fulcrum Press collection out of Fisher's ad-hoc emergence as a poet that set the stage for *City*'s being taken up as his signature work. The critical writings on it by Davie and Mottram, as well as individual essays by Peter Barry and others listed in the secondary bibliography, then confirmed both its distinctiveness and role in providing the poet with a literary identity. The slightly misleading impression given by *Collected Poems 1968* is, after all, that the poems in *City* are not 'early poems', though they are from the same period as some from the first section, or that Fisher had written a few trial pieces and then blossomed out with this unusual combination of prose and poetry, a work which could claim then, and still can, to be a uniquely significant literary response to the demolition and rebuilding of the urban centres of non-metropolitan England. We know it to be derived from Birmingham, but that identity is not signalled in the published work, and in interview Fisher would call it a city of the mind.

Yet it would be wrong if the story told here were to suggest that *City* had come to take its place in Fisher's work only by a series of accidents. Rather it is an example of the ways in which the making of art is not necessarily only a 'lonely writer' activity, but a collaborative process. It also shows how the lineaments of a literary work and the profile of its writer may be created by the exigencies of publication and reception. Trials and errors, happy and unhappy rejections have their part to play. Behind it lies the determination of the writer to preserve the good qualities of some early writing from contamination by other impulses that do not promise a direction for development, and to bring together various separate promptings into an ensemble whose whole is mysteriously so much greater than the sum of its parts.

4. Understanding *City*

As is clear from the process of trial and error outlined above, not only did Fisher not plan *City*, but he allowed it to be launched into the world with a Preface that declared it a 'ruined work of art'. Shayer's introductory prose is then the first attempt to understand what had emerged from this collaging of prose passages written for a different purpose and independent poems not intended to form part of a larger whole. That process also left Fisher with a work that he had himself to come to understand, not least if he was to extend and revise it, and we see him beginning and reporting on such an understanding in correspondence with Turnbull and Davie above.

The large number of authorial comments on *City* excerpted below not only testify to its signature position in Fisher's oeuvre, but to the amount of thought he would put into its understanding once completed. It is hardly an exaggeration that this process continued for much of the poet's creative life, and certainly played its part in the conception of *A Furnace* a quarter of a century later. On 11 June 2000, his 70th birthday, Fisher began a new notebook with the following observation:

> Backwash from the three books. When [Tom] Maschler asked me for a collection in 65 I had to work through the summer to add enough items to the miscellany to make a book. It never occurred to me to reprint *City*; and it was only after Cape had rejected and Stuart [Montgomery] was trying to bulk out the book that he came up with the suggestion of hanging the book on it. And that enabled me to discard elements in the Cape submission. Cape, I suppose, said no because the MS had no handle – auto-biography, war – whereas Stuart could see that *City* would provide one.

In the next entry, written on 14 June, a Wednesday, he adds:

> That showed me – and there'd been the Sara Golden New York hawl, for which I'd sent more or less the same miscellany of aesthetic bids – that, since I worked by following my uncertain nose and without strategy or ego-drive, I was miles from where a publisher might be thinking. Then there's the matter of the principles of exclusion in *CP 1968*.

Those principles are now outlined in 'Roy Fisher on the Nature of Neglect', his candid and witty Afterword to *Slakki*, where he notes that his 'contribution was to add a level of self-censorship' to effect 'at once an introduction and a valediction' produced 'with an eye to the vicious reviewing climate of the time', a climate characterised and mocked by 'The Making of the Book', one of only two poems Fisher wrote in 1967 from within the writing block that appears to have descended under the weight of an emerging sense that his writings had readers.

Sara Golden, who worked at Pantheon Books, had apparently solicited a typescript that also failed to reach publication. These 'backwash' retrospections by the poet at his 70th birthday had been prompted by the publication of *Interviews Through Time and Selected Prose*, edited by Tony Frazer (Shearsman Books), *News for the Ear: A Homage to Roy Fisher*, edited by Robert Sheppard and me (Stride Publications), and *The Thing about Roy Fisher: Critical Studies*, edited by John Kerrigan and me again (Liverpool University Press). These three books, in their different ways, recognise a poet with a biography, an oeuvre, and a trajectory, none of which were or evidently felt by that author to be true of the non-metropolitan writer finding his way in the later 1950s and early 1960s. The tale of how *City* came to be this poet's signature work took place, then, against the grain of that writer 'following my uncertain nose and without strategy or ego-drive'. And this certainly helps explain the nature of the materials from which it emerged.

One way to understand *City*, then, might be to see it as the assertion of an artistic motivation which requires a certain amount of focused subjectivity to give it a direction, even if this subjectivity is a device for accessing, and focusing on, the cultural and historical materials that are its real concern. Thus, there are the autobiographical elements about which Fisher expressed so much suspicion, foremost among them 'The Entertainment of War'; but they could also include the tonally coherent and consistently voiced early prose passages, which provide a documentary-like establishing shot. The first poem, the 'Lullaby and Exhortation for the Unwilling Hero', is a bluntly estranging device which informs us that this work will not be a piece of social realism, even if the unwilling hero, a ghost of the Citizen, perhaps, might seem to align the work with the angry young men of northern realism emerging at the same moment in fiction, cinema and music. Yet the subsequent return to substantial prose passages pondering the form and experience of the city means that even Fisher's claim in interview that he was intending a city of the mind does not quite catch the never entirely settled mode of the work. No sooner has a reader taken on the idea that it will have a surreally modernist poetic texture than it returns to its documentary voice-over mode, only then to catch up imagist urban or song-like lyrics in its mix.

The Migrant *City* is a work that illustrates the 'ruined'

claim of the Preface by establishing such hybrid registers and mode-shifting, but it fails to take them to anywhere like a destination. The necessary point of arrival in the revision is then provided by the I-directed prose passages that lead towards the definitive work's close. The experiences of the city differently presented in the various versions of its anthological assemblage have, however much Fisher might have temperamentally resisted it, a subject figure by which they can be registered and within which they may be understood as forming a problem or predicament. For there is a political and cultural critique emerging from the work, one which is, at this stage, only able to be accessed indirectly, by following its nose – an evolving critique which would come to be articulated and elaborated in *A Furnace*. Nor is it an exaggeration to suggest that Fisher's later masterpiece, as its 'Introit' hints, grew out of what he eventually understood himself to have stumbled upon, as it were, by collaging together in various iterations these poems and passages of prose a quarter of a century before.

The troubled subject of the closing prose paragraphs in the definitive version of *City* does have his problems, his wanting to believe he lives in a single world, for instance, and they are differently exemplified in the 'Hallucinations' material that Fisher would remove, and in the dreamlike or disturbed identifications and reflections he retained. These issues are differently figured in the displaced social collaboration exemplified by 'Starting to Make a Tree' and the concluding exhortation of 'The Park'. Read aright, *City* can tell us a great deal about the emergence of the kinds of half-modernised, and half-ruined, hybridised, collaged, richly poor urban environments in which so many British people were, and still are, obliged to thrive or survive. It can tell us a lot too about the strategies of reality-testing and fantasy-projection to which its citizens would resort so as to get by in these complexly nondescript by-products of the country's largely now posthumous heavy-industrial prosperity.

The ur-materials out of which Fisher's definitive version emerged are presented here for the illumination that they bring to the various acts of artful selectivity that went into the composition of this collage. They also cast into fresh relief the continuing importance of Fisher's signature work, and how it came to form a whole more significant than the sum of its parts. For if the poet could write of the urban environments that were inspiring his writings around the dawning of the 1960s that 'most of it has never been seen', this is as true of what's presented in *The Citizen*, the selection of related, uncollected poems, and the variant versions of *City*. Fisher's intent was never only to enable these places to be seen. Like Joseph Conrad he wanted to let us see, and that of course means under-stand. Seeing what he first saw and then left out will, I hope, be a help in understanding exactly what, by follow-ing his nose, Roy Fisher was, through these trials and this testing, eventually enabled to have us see.

THE CITIZEN

(1959)

I

1.

On one of the steep slopes that rise towards the centre
of the city all the buildings have been destroyed within
the last year: a whole district of tall narrow houses that
spilled around what were, a hundred years ago, outlying
factories, has gone. The streets remain among the rough
quadrilaterals of brick-rubble, veering awkwardly towards
one another through nothing; at night their rounded
surfaces still shine under the irregularly-set gaslamps, and
tonight they dully reflect also the yellowish flare, diffused
and baleful, that hangs flat in the clouds a few hundred
feet above the city's invisible heart. Occasional cars move
cautiously across this waste, as if suspicious of the emptiness;
there is little to separate the roadways from what lies
between them. Their tail-lights vanish slowly into the
blocks of surrounding buildings, maybe a quarter of a mile
from the middle of the desolation.

And what is it that lies between the purposeless streets?
There is not a whole brick, a foundation to stumble across,
a drainpipe, a smashed fowl house; the entire place has
been razed flat, dug over, and smoothed down again. The
bald curve of the hillside shows quite clearly here, near its
crown, where the brilliant road, stacked close on either side
with warehouses and shops, runs out towards the west.
Down below, the district that fills the hollow is impenetrably
black. The streets there are so close and so twisted among
their massive tenements that it is impossible to trace the
line of a single one of them by its lights. The lamps that

can be seen shine oddly, and at mysterious distances, as if they were in a marsh. Only the great flat-roofed factory shows clear by its bulk, stretching across three or four whole blocks just below the edge of the waste, with solid rows of lit windows.

Uncovered here is the hard bone the city is raised on. Yet it is a ground so moist and treacherous that subways cannot be cut through it.

2.

On the station platform, near a pile of baskets, a couple embraced, pressed close together and swaying a little. It was hard to see where the girl's feet and legs were. The suspicion this aroused soon caused her hands, apparently joined behind her lover's back, to become a small brown-paper parcel under the arm of a stout engine driver who leaned, probably drunk, against the baskets, his cap so far forward as almost to conceal his face. I could not banish from my mind the thought that what I had first seen was in fact his own androgynous fantasy, the self-sufficient core of his stupor. Such a romantic thing, so tender, for him to contain. He looked more comic and complaisant than the couple had done; and more likely to fall heavily to the floor.

3.

A man in the police court. He looked dapper and poker-faced, his arms straight, the long fingers just touching the hem of his checked jacket. Four days after being released from the prison where he had served two years for theft he had been discovered at midnight clinging like a tree-shrew to the bars of a glass factory-roof. He made no attempt to explain his presence there; the luminous nerves that made him fly up to it were not visible in daylight and the police seemed hardly able to believe this was the creature they had brought down in the darkness.

If I could climb on to the slate-roof of my house now I could see the towers of the jail where he is.

4.

I am always glad to hear of a death, even if it grieves me; and miserable to learn of any performance of the sexual act. I read the obituaries in the newspaper eagerly; each of these stopped lives becomes comprehensible, and submits to the agencies of fermentation, distortions of the will, my will that lives only in my memories – without being able any longer to struggle. From the carved or printed epitaph, the few bundles of clumsy and broken outlines that remain, I can breed whatever I want.

Yet whenever I am forced to realise that some of these people around me, people I have actually seen, whose hopeful and distended surface I have at moments touched, are bodily in love and express that love bodily to dying-point, I feel that it is my own energy, my own hope, tension and sense of time in hand, that have gathered and vanished down that dark drain; that it is I who am left, shivering and exhausted, to try and kick the lid back into place so that I can go on without fear. And the terror that fills that moment or hour while I do it is a terror of anaesthesia: being able to feel only vertically, like a blind wall, or thickly, like the tyres of a bus.

Lovers turn to me faces of innocence where I would rather see faces of bright cunning. They have disappeared for entire hours into the lit holes of life, instead of lying stunned on its surface as I, and so many do for so long; or instead of raising their heads cautiously and scenting the manifold airs that blow through the streets. Sex fuses the intersections of the web where it occurs into blobs that drag and stick; and the web is not made to stand such weights. Often, there is no web.

5.

Sitting in the dark, I see a window, a large sash window of four panes such as might be found in the living room of any fair-sized old house. Its curtains are drawn back and it looks out on to a small damp garden, narrow close at hand where the kitchen and outhouses lead back, and then almost square. It is surrounded by privet and box, and the flowerbeds are empty save for a few laurels or rhododendrons, some leafless rose-shrubs and a giant yucca. It is a December afternoon, and it is raining. Not far from the window is a black marble statue of a long-haired, long-bearded old man. His robes are conventionally archaic, and he sits, easily enough, on what seems a pile of small boulders, staring intently and with a look of great intelligence, towards the patch of wall just under the kitchen window. The statue looks grimy, but its exposed surfaces are highly polished by the rain, so that the nose and the cheekbones stand out strongly in the gloom. It is rather smaller than life-size. It is clearly not in its proper place; resting as it does across the moss of the raised border, it is appreciably tilted forward and to one side, almost as if it had been abandoned as too heavy by those who were trying to move it – either in or out.

6.

In the century since this city has become great, it has twice laid itself out in the shape of a wheel. The ghost of the older one still lies among the spokes of the new, those dozen loud highways that thread constricted ways through the inner suburbs, then thrust out, twice as wide, across the housing estates and into the countryside, dragging moraines of buildings with them. Sixty or seventy years ago there were other main roads, quite as important as these were then, but lying between their paths. By day, they are simply alternatives, short cuts, lined solidly with parked cars and crammed with delivery vans. They look merely like side-streets, heartlessly overblown in some excess of Victorian expansion. By night, or on a Sunday, you can see them for what they are. They are still lit by gas, and the long rows of houses, three and four storeys high, rear black above the lamps, enclosing the roadways, damping them off from whatever surrounds them. From these pavements you can sometimes see the sky at night, not obscured as it is in most parts of the city by the greenish-blue haze of light that steams out of the mercury-vapour lamps. These streets are not worth lighting. The houses have not been turned into shops – they are not villas either, that might have been offices, but simply tall dwellings, opening straight off the street, with cavernous entries leading into back courts.

The people who live in them are mostly very old. Some have lived through three wars, some through only one: wars of newspapers, of mysterious sciences, of coercion, of disappearances. Wars that have come down the streets from the unknown city and the unknown world, like rain-water floods in the gutters. There are small shops at street corners, with whole faceless rows of houses between them; and public houses carved only shallowly into the massive walls. When these people go into the town, the buses they travel on stop just before they reach it, in the sombre back streets behind the Town Hall and the great insurance offices, or in the few streets that manage, on the southern side, to cross the imperious lines of the railway that fan out on broad viaducts from their tunnels beneath the central hill.

These lost streets are decaying only very slowly. The impacted lives of their inhabitants, the meaninglessness of news, the dead black of the chimney breasts, the conviction that the wind itself comes only from the next street, all wedge together to keep destruction out, to deflect the eye of the developer. And when destruction comes it is total: printed notices on the walls, block by block, a few doors left open at night, broken windows advancing down a street until fallen slates appear on the pavement and are not kicked away. Then, after a few weeks of this, the machines arrive.

7.

A café with a frosted glass door through which much light is diffused. A tall young girl comes out and stands in front of it, her face and figure quite obscured by this milky radiance.

She treads out on to a lopsided ochre panel of pavement before the doorway, and becomes visible as a coloured shape, moving sharply. A wrap of honey and ginger, a flared saffron skirt, grey-white shoes. She goes off past the Masonic Temple with a young man: he is pale, with dark hair and a shrunken, earnest face. One could imagine him a size larger. Just for a moment, as it happens, there is no one else in the street at all. Their significance escapes rapidly like a scent, before the footsteps vanish among the car engines.

8.

Cannot complain. There is no cause for complaint. There is no ground for complaint. No audience for complaint. No comprehension of complaint. There is no language for complaint. There is no possibility of complaint. Complaint does not exist.

9.

In this city the governing authority is limited and mean; so limited that it can do no more than preserve a superficial order. It supplies fuel, water and power. It removes a fair proportion of the refuse, cleans the streets after a fashion and discourages fighting. With these few things it is content. This could never be a capital city, for all its size. There is no mind in it, no regard. The sensitive, the tasteful, the fashionable, the intolerant and powerful have not moved through it as they have moved through London, evaluating it, altering deliberately, setting in motion wars of feeling about it. Most of it has never been seen.

10.

There are photographs taken by long exposure of streets by night. In them the lights of windows and streetlamps show as motionless blobs; but the pictures are dominated by the tangled confusion of smears and lines made by the lights of moving buses and cars, bright marks that have no clear beginnings or ends; some of them make strange curves and loops on the edges of the maze, but always return to it. Sometimes life here resembles such a picture; a mass of blind and contorted purposes that cannot be separated or understood. There is never one which rears up in pain and remains, cut off where it stands, for the gestures of tragedy are caught early by watchful ambulances, policewomen and newspaper reporters, who all know how to neutralise them quickly and efficiently, discharging them after treatment into the foggy gully of the public memory.

'When you begin to remember, when you think for a moment that you can taste the chimney pots or can conjure the scent of umbrellas on your breath – take a bus, greet new friends, remember you can read.

'There has been a major war since then. Things are constantly appearing in a new light. It is to be presumed that the children are enabled to see it.

'When the figures on the calendar change it becomes more than evident that something has happened that must affect us all.'

I am not dying or mad; my crimes are minor and not easily detectable; there is little about me that would divert or scandalise the public; so my thoughts have not yet fallen into the hands of the hospitals, the police or the press. Yet they are the thoughts of a tragedy: of the defiance of life. They are so now, when I cannot recognise anything that I see, when I know that all things that I encounter are extensions of my own body; I cannot even recognise that. They tend upwards to breaking point, in a landscape of destroyed war engines curving romantically into a smooth sky – today. Left lying a day, they'll curve their ends round with curative gestures and become in some sense comic – the sense of shapes contained within other shapes contained within life. The tragic knows, while it briefly exists, that life cannot satisfactorily contain it.

II

11.

The release is coming. I am going to be able to die. With that ability in my pocket I shall be able to use the past.

The spit turns, or the stage revolves. With a sudden tumble and grating, with a certain diabolic suction of music, I am given a new set of faces, new symbols to bear. The setting is quite particular. Where I was born, on the edge of the city a narrow road runs north from the main westward road into the small triangle of farmland that still separates the city from two of its neighbouring townships. After a couple of hundred yards it is joined by what was once a lane but is now the last of the suburban streets. It has houses on one side and a cemetery on the other. Between the main road and this lane, called Cole Lane, a large laundry was built in about 1930: a low brick building lying back from the roadway behind spiked railings and perfunctory gardens of lawn and laurel. The corner opposite the cemetery gate is now the laundry's car park; but before the war there was still the small yard of a monumental stonemason called McLean. It had a lean-to office with wide windows, a three-legged hoist with a dangling hook, and a neatly gravelled patch, fenced off with loops of tarred chain between short marble posts, in which the completed tombstones were displayed for sale.

In this vanished place I see my images, casually disposed among the marble carpentry. There are four of them lying there; and perhaps the little yard itself makes a fifth, unlike the others in that I have seen it before – though I have probably not thought of it for twenty years.

The four things are greyish white, corpse-colour. Indeed the most arresting of them is the figure of a woman, quite nude, lying stiffly on the side of the gravel between the polished headstones, looking as if she had been tipped there after the limbs had grown rigid. The others are what appears to be an albino raven lying similarly, with folded wings; a neat pile of coke ash and clinker; and a man's cotton singlet, clean but frayed into holes at the hem. This vest is as such a garment might be, soft and light; the wind flutters it where it lies draped. The ashes too are visibly loose and of a natural texture though somewhat bleached. But the woman and the bird seem stony and hard, like a waxworks or petrified things.

The woman is tall and lean, not beautiful. A flat narrow belly, breasts that are hardly noticeable; a stringy, athletic physique. The shoulders are high and square, the face supercilious and a little mean, with a nose that curves strongly over a long upper lip and a poor chin. There is no expression and the eyes are shut as in an unguarded sleep.

The hair, quite fair and straight, is fastened close to the head in a kind of plait, such as a sternly-reared little girl might wear. It is a body that has been put under strain by the will.

The bird – I do not know so much about birds: it may be a jackdaw, not a raven. It is quite large, with ragged feathers and knobbly claws. But it has a great smoothness and dignity in its lack of colour; the beak and eyes are lightly closed and the head inclined a little forwards. This is the least welcome of the four.

The ashes make a roughly conical pile six or eight inches high. They seem to be the product of an unusual heat. Some marble chippings have got in amongst them, and there are faint gleams from streaks of fused metal.

As for the vest, it is merely the sort of undergarment I have worn in winter through most of my life; though it is clearly of a small size. Cheap in the first place and now clearly worn to a state where it would be too thin for warmth and too ragged for comfort.

These objects are unlike the warmer, more animate images that have been my companions before. They are much closer. They are made for a stillness that forces my regard and for a permanence that exacts my respect. 'Now you are here,' I imagine them saying. They imply, too, that all this has been a long while in coming: I confront them not in the guise in which I came along this actual lane at nineteen, ten years ago, dispossessed, frightened, at ease in the unruly countryside, but in that of a respectable householder of the neighbourhood, a soberly dressed man whose walking here is to be regarded as a quiet eccentricity or a reconnaissance of Authority.

Can this be my fate? A handful of things that takes so

little account of myself, my beginnings, my circumstances, my early imaginings? They are shapes of hatred, with the hatred gone.

Now the sun pours gold over the tombstones, over the bird's chill feathers, over the woman's stone groin. They sink a little way in my vision. I can sense myself standing closer, standing over them; they glitter with my pity, for I cannot know them to be my creatures without feeling compassion. But this sunlight that wavers across them – I cannot tell its strength or its season – is a new sunlight: nothing warm, fluid, dispersing, but a razor or a sheet of glass.

I am in my home. This is where I came, year by year, into the world. The four seasons first showed themselves in the scrubby hedges of these two lanes; this matter is my measure of time, the people I shall meet if I walk here are to me the calendars of the body. How can it have harboured these horrors that I must at last call beautiful?

I shall easily survive this dilation of the here and now. That much is certain. And it is certain that I must some-how nurse these things. It is as if I should be forced to remove them to a place less exposed, more private, carry-ing them under my coat, in a travelling bag, crated up and pushed on a handcart through the crowds of men and women disgorged at midday from the laundry and the factories that lie on the further side of the main road.

In thinking of ways of removing them I find myself planning automatically to take them to my old home, my parents' house. There they could have the room that used to be mine, taking their places with the dismantled bed that stands against the wall, the empty wardrobe, the two straight chairs stacked neatly, one upside down upon the other. Would they be as terrible to the old people as the thought that visited me so often in childhood – the thought of living with the dead body of my mother or my father in the house, awaiting burial?

As to how they came to that yard on the corner: maybe I have put them there. Every loss of dead matter from my body has gathered together to form them. It may be that it was only my nails, my hair, my worn skin; it may have been everything. This is the figure of my death. I will not say redemption. If I cease to feel their presence, I will know I have ceased to feel.

12.

The centre of the city, so tightly cramped for generations about a lopsided triangle of streets, is shaking itself and growing, almost visibly. Every week the traffic has to learn different ways as old streets are barricaded with chestnut palings and corrugated iron sheets, and stretches of new roadway are unceremoniously put into use as soon as the builders' hoardings are dismantled. The stone faced, crouching Victorian blocks that line the main streets are being quietly destroyed, hastily and almost without announcement; a shop or a café may disappear into a dusty void if left unvisited for a month. I thought I knew these streets, but I can remember little of what has gone, for there are too many names, too many locations to learn for the first time in the last weeks before their demolition. And few of these places have been hospitable; mostly they have grinned too glassily. Yet I am surprised to find them less permanent than I. When some of these brutal and coquettish structures were blown up in the bombing it did not seem unusual or improper; but to see men hammering away the cornices, lifting out windows, hauling the remains of thick walls into heaps is strange. These buildings do not stand separate, as if capable of being isolated and removed; they squat shoulder to shoulder, their heavily decorated crests of an even height above the roadway, from one street through to the next in what seems an impregnable mass covering as much as an acre. And the whole acre is laid bare. To protect passers by, great sheets of canvas in blotched shades of green and brown are hung down in a ghastly patchwork across the building's face.

I remember walking up a side street towards the Listowel Hotel, a blank, pale building that occupied almost the whole side of the street into which this one led. I knew it had been deserted for weeks and was used to the sight of the shuttered doors and the windows robbed of all personality; but now, when I came within sight of it I was confronted only with this huge wall of dirty canvas sodden and bellying in the rain, like the flank of a monstrous and diseased creature. On the corner, a couple of bare windows stared out, but there was no sign at all of whatever was being done inside.

Often, on these devastated sites, a part of the new building is begun before the destruction of the old is complete. There is a place at the end of the main street, where the land falls sharply away to the southward, towards the river above which the old town spread gradually along the hill. The slope is at last visible, for here most of the buildings have gone; and across the street a great gap has been cut across the shopping centre. From this one point can be seen all of the seven giant cranes that tower over the district, turning rigidly at odd angles among the rising walls.

Some of the new buildings are already finished and in

use. A few are as much as two or three years old, bored and beginning to look grimy. All of them are huge, white, angular and purposeful, glittering with enormous panes, rearing expressionless heads over the huddled streets among which they have been fitted with so much difficulty. With their arcades and smooth vistas, they act on the body like diminishing lenses, making it smaller, but more precise, pert, confident.

13.

Late in July, three-thirty in the afternoon, by the entrance to the central Post Office. A hot day, with a little wind, a breath in the streets. A detectable lull in the movement of people across the pavements; the eddies of the crowd slowing and beginning to curdle. I walked through the revolving door and down the steps, and found that these movements had thickened at one point into immobility. A girl was standing firmly in the middle of the pavement, obstructing it. Her head raised, she was talking to a tall man who had his back to me. He was still – poised easily, as if in the act of walking: she seemed set there to stay, not budging when jostled by those who passed.

Her head was striking. The straight nose lay close to the face, and clamped a kind of strength into the upper lip. Then, as she laughed and spoke to the companion who bent courteously over her, I saw the whiteness and evenness of her teeth, the firm chin, and the energy of the entire face.

Strange eyes; well set but narrowed by the high cheekbones and the low, straight brow. The eyebrows, like the hair were a coppery red, well marked and almost furry, and the thick hair, caught up in an uneven swath, grew low on the forehead. These things combined to give her the air of a clean and forceful animal which lived, not as a human being, through eyes and brain, but through muscles, bones and mouth.

She was dressed rather aggressively in a checked frock of black and white, stiffly cut and tight-bodiced, held in at the waist by a broad red belt. Most of her effect came from the head, which was a trifle large; and her vivacity was of such a kind that it was not at first apparent that she was above the average in height – the tallness of her companion helped to conceal this.

What made her more than merely fetching, though, and made the paving slabs around her come alive like a stage floor, and the passers-by begin to walk far enough away to be able to stare at her, was the thick, opaque whiteness of her skin; for all her animation, not a flush disturbed this matt pallor, which gave a theatrical self-possession to the whole appearance.

It was after seeing her thus that I realised who her companion was.

Extremely well dressed in a relaxed way, courteous and still heavily handsome, though the traces of his latent insanity were beginning to be apparent in the set of his hunched shoulders as well as in the grotesque remoteness of his face whenever he was not consciously controlling his expression, he was making a festival of the town, giving a niche in history to everyone who passed through the square that afternoon, painting the sunlight of a pioneer photographer's time-exposure on to the green lamp-standards and the tarmac. I sensed the last beribboned horses coming in past the refreshment tent; the dismantling of the floral tableaux; the crowds drifting to kill time before the firework display and seeing, inescapably, the dusty mechanism of the afternoon's entertainment. By next week he would be gone.

At five minutes to twelve that night they were standing at a bus stop under the concrete awning of a department store; he was paying off a taxi and, in the deserted street, only just left by the sweepers, they were still being charming to each other.

A pair of lovers. Did she have the look of bright cunning or that of innocence? In the afternoon the one; in the night the other, probably – or so I would see it. He had neither. Madeley is not innocent, except in the perverse reaches of his faith. He is not innocent with the girl; whatever he relinquishes into women it is not his face, his eyes. His cunning is not bright, but is huge and impersonal, something that broods uneasily among the sunlit roofs of the tall white buildings that I sometimes feel he conveys into the city from those absences of his which he loves.

Years ago, when I first knew him, he walked in a city of such buildings, before it began to take shape, before there was any hint that they would be raised. A city made of the sort of dreams people had before the war. He ignored the conservatism of the war (in his boyhood) and of the solid, impoverished despair that followed it, seeing no reason why dreams so positive should be rejected – 'discredited'. Now that it is all happening, now he can, whenever he returns, walk through the curved subways of his own mind while they are still clean and have not grown habitually invisible, he must be more conscious of his body, of the effects of time upon it. It no longer looks like a body that will remember love.

14.

The edge of the city. A low hill with houses on one side and rough common land on the other, stretching down to where a dye-works lies along the valley road. Pithead gears thrust out above the hawthorn bushes; everywhere prefabricated workshops jut into the fields and the allotments. The society of singing birds and the society of mechanical hammers inhabit the world together, slightly ruffled and confused by each other's presence.

15.

Once I wanted to prove the world was sick. Now I want to prove it healthy. The detection of sickness means that death has established itself as an element of the timetable; it has come within the range of the measurable. Where there is no time there is no sickness.

One afternoon I walked along the rickety boardwalk that had replaced the pavement outside the Listowel while it was being demolished. It was narrow, bounded on one side by a yellow hoarding and on the other by an iron scaffolding over which the lower edges of the canvas curtain hung. Two people could just pass. Halfway along this I found myself giving way to a tall elderly woman who stared straight ahead, softly, and made no effort to accommodate herself to the shuffling files of men and women. She was thin, and dingily dressed, and her complexion was livid, a dirty vegetable colour that I had never seen in flesh before. To walk anywhere must have been for her an effort that almost destroyed consciousness. Her neck, from the throat of her jacket to the ear, was encased in a support of plastic or rubber, rigid like the tubing of an enormous gas-mask, and of a subdued, rubbed, yellowish-grey. I drew back, and she passed.

Weeks later in the shopping street of a suburb four or five miles away, I caught a glimpse of her, similarly brief, between two vans parked across the street.

Those two moments were the same, or interchangeable. They could be piled one on the other, like pennies. To me she was horrible and fascinating but not sick in the sense that she exacted my concern. Had we met, had we then possessed any common language, I would willingly have talked to her of war, of food, of children, of death. I would not have wished to hear of the movements of her disease. Had she insisted on bringing it into the conversation, I would have felt obliged to mention my own disease, which is hereditary, complete in its domination of me, progressive, so slow as to be barely perceptible. But as I saw her, knowing nothing except what I saw, the two moments were the same; as there were two, I had to pile them.

When, though, I saw Madeley and the girl at the bus stop that night, I could not help putting the two moments in which I encountered them end to end in a fixed sequence, with only the slightest overlap. There was no real need for this: merely on the evidence of what I saw the night could well have preceded the day. I did it because of what I thought I knew, that third moment in which I was not present, and whose image made me suppose in the girl's face a surrender (a defeat, and abdication from self) which may not have been there.

16.

I have stood, looking over this city from the little waste plain above where the curving railway bites its long sour furrow up into the west.

I have seen the city as a bowl filled with peace, its nearby turbulence of lines, pangs of dark terraces, softened among the fading reaches.

I have seen the solid roofs' tideway fingering points of light through wintry haze.

I have seen the spots of blood on the soft feathers of its wings.

17.

I have thought of those wings as the wings of a gull that might come here in winter, flapping in from the coast a hundred miles away, congregating with others on green playing fields and the untended recesses of the parks in the suburbs; I have thought of them as the wings of a pigeon, awake bleak-eyed before the human dawn, a bird from one of those flocks that wheel dazzling above the crowded roofs; I have thought of them as the wings of a dove, that has no place here.

My bird, my unwelcome albino raven that has appeared at last, is not one of the city's living birds: sparrows, starlings, pigeons, a few thrushes and blackbirds on the outskirts, robins in the larger gardens are all we have – and the fancy waterfowl on the park ponds. Yet this petrified freak is the bird of my city, my bird for this place. It would not have come to me anywhere else.

The city could have produced it from within itself; it is spacious enough, secret enough. There are suburbs I have never properly visited, or have never managed to find recognisable as I have passed through them, districts that melt into one another without climax. In one of these, in a side road out of a side road, this bird might have been bred and manufactured, in a large shed running the whole length of a garden that is cut off by the high wall of an old timberyard or repair shop. By whom? A small family business in the last stages of decay; the father, the most confused son, the least responsible uncle. The father sixty, short and quick, with baggy overalls, a scrawny, mobile neck, a small round head with stiff grey hair brushed upwards even at the back, and little fat lips. The son, nearly thirty, just married; taller than the father, but similar, with a weak neck and hollower cheeks. His hair is fair, like the brows and lashes of his singularly puffy eyes. The uncle, in his fifties, and unmarried, is crablike and stout with a lined reddish face and very dark hair, quite wavy.

It is possible that they supply pet-shops; or maybe they make garden ornaments of cement or creosoted logs: bird tables, rustic seats, gnomes, rabbits, toadstools. In some crisis or exhaustion, or exultation, lost for a while to the sense of the world, they may have produced my bird without realising it.

What is it? Napoleon. Goethe. A stillborn ruler for the city. Cold, large-headed, enormously wise, completely immobile.

It is important that it was born through these people, or through me, without any sort of Annunciation. Anything here that is publicly announced is rapidly destroyed by the million familiar little glances of the people. The things that are themselves, that go to make the body of the city, are unannounced, are made without full consultation or advice, without consideration for feeling. The new buildings are part of that body for the moment, while they are incomplete, because the power that raises them is a force of such complete and unscrupulous cupidity that the press has no vocabulary for describing it. Financially, it is possible that the work might be brought to a standstill and never continued; the town might be left half-disembowelled, a possibility so monstrous that no one considers it. And the speculators go on gambling.

The bird is the poetry of the city that nobody has ever dared speak. The poetry of the unseen colossus that lies hidden among countless lights. It is unwelcome in the same way that tea-leaves in a cup are unwelcome; it has a similar flavour of bitterness, origin and command. I resent its inscrutability, the suspicion I have that it may be worthless, the doubts I have about whether it is moral or sensual. It reveals no taste whatever. In that, certainly, it is like a part of the natural world. I thought at first that it was so obviously literary, so hoarily embedded in the symbolism of the last century that I could account it an aberration and so dismiss it, but its urbane banality is clearly something I must have been desiring. With the other three things only, I should have been too comfortable, and too lonely: a woman, a heap of ashes, a vest – I could have been a Crusoe within myself. Slowly, this bird and I are working on each other. The only rule in our game is that neither of us must appear to change.

18.

At the time when the great streets were carelessly and, it now seems, effortlessly, thrust out along the ancient highways and trackways, the tall houses shouldering solidly towards the country and the back streets filling in the widening spaces between them like webbed membranes, the power of will in the town was more openly confident, less speciously democratic, than it is now. There were, of course, cottage railway stations, a jail that pretended to be a castle out of Grimm, public urinals surrounded by screens of cast iron lacework painted green and scarlet; but there was also an arrogant and ponderous architecture that dwarfed and terrified the people by its sheer size and functional brutality: the workhouses and the older hospitals, the thick-walled abattoir, the long vaulted market halls, the striding canal bridges and railway viaducts. Brunel was welcome here. Compared with these structures the straight white blocks and concrete roadways of today are a fairground, a clear dream just before waking, the creation of salesmen rather than engineers. The new city is bred out of a hard will, but as it appears it shows itself a little ingratiating, a place of arcades, passages, easy ascents, good light. The eyes twinkle, beseech and veil themselves; the full, hard mouth, the broad jaw – these are no longer made visible to all.

A street a mile long with no buildings, only a continuous embankment of sick grass along one side with railway signals on it and strings of trucks through whose black-spoked wheels you can see the sky; and, for the whole length of the other a curving wall of smooth bluish brick, caked with soot and thirty feet high. In it, a few wicket gates painted ochre and fingermarked, but never open. Cobbles in the roadway.

A hundred years ago this was the edge of town. The goods yards, the gasworks and the coal stores were established on tips and hillocks in the sparse fields that lay among the thinning houses. Between this place and the centre, a mile or two away up the hill, lay a continuous huddle of low streets and courts, filling the marshy valley of the meagre river that now flows in a culvert under the brick and tarmac. The two main lines came curving in round the hill which confronts the town across the valley. Then they had to leap. The feet of the viaducts were planted down among the streets. One of the tracks was soon taken across into the hillside, tunnelling under the main streets and coming out at the other edge: the other stopped as soon as it reached the rising slope. A great station was built, towering, stucco-fronted, stony. The sky above it was southerly. The stately approach, the long curves of yellow wall, still remain; but the place is a goods depot with most of its doors barred and homely pots of geraniums at those windows that are not shuttered. You come upon it suddenly in its open prospect out of tangled streets of small factories. It draws light to itself, especially at sunset, standing still and smooth faced, looking westward up the hill. Yet I am not able to imagine the activity that must once have been here. I can see no ghosts of men and women, only the gigantic ghost of stone. They are too frightened of it to pull it down.

19.

The ashes are simply what is left. There is always something, and it is always a relic, even after only a moment. Something to be touched, to be handled hopelessly; something that obeys the laws of matter even before it is subjected to chance and the speculative will.

There was a time when myths were very real to me and I would skirt the colliery spoilbank that stands in the fields beside a wide reedy pond with swans and moorhens on it, half expecting to see, among the colours streaks of ash, purple, orange and black, the figure of Lancelot or

Gawain lying uncovered, naked, made of fired white porcelain decorated with flowers, and with hand or shin or phallus snapped off and lost, like a handle. Or a sizeable splinter of the True Cross, almost undistinguishable among the singed brown shale. Those slopes are so quickly fissured by rain and so baleful in colour that they can seem, especially near water, immeasurably ancient, volcanic.

20.

The men who are demolishing the old buildings say they have to be very careful when selling rubble to the contractors for the new. The brickwork of a factory may well be chemically so rotted and altered as to be unusable.

21.

I went to two schools in the city. I can think of nine of my schoolfellows who are now dead. Only one is a girl: Jill Shavers, when she was nearly thirty, fell from the motorcycle on which she was a passenger and was killed.

Derek Ashmore died of leukemia when he was seven. A mean, sneering, greedy boy, distorted by those who knew he would not live. We children all paid pennies to buy a vile purple wreath for his funeral.

Donald Hayward. Actor, clown, philanderer. He looked like Grimaldi, would never, they said, have passed his examinations. Aged sixteen, he died in three weeks of some sort of paralysis.

Kenneth Lowe. A spindly boy with a thin sharp nose, and egg-head, sleepy eyes. I last saw him at sixteen. He played football for an Old Boys' team for seven years after that. Then he was kicked on his abnormally thin skull and died there on the field.

Leon Costoe. An agile little boy, unkempt and pugnacious. He was taken with his platoon for first lessons in swimming to a public baths in St Helen's and drowned in the shallow end. Nobody saw the body lying on the bottom until they lined up to leave.

Michael Wills. Seventeen, with an artificial reserve and dignity. Travelling home from a school camp he leaned out of the back of the van to whistle at two girls. He was thrown out and fractured his skull; after that he lived for three weeks or so, unconscious.

John Slade was walking one night with a girl near his Airforce camp when a lorry passing at great speed struck him, injuring him terribly. The girl was untouched, the lorry never traced.

Anthony Goldner drove his car at speed into the parapet of a high river bridge a few months after his mother's death.

Howard Lewis. The brilliant and sadistic. He hanged himself carefully from the banister one summer evening while his parents were out visiting. He was fifteen.

Almost certainly there are more than these: deaths I have not heard of. Three of these I learned of deviously, long after they occurred. I chanced on two more looking at a local newspaper I saw only rarely.

22.

I have found ways of moving through this town where so many people know me without meeting any of them. In a week there are many times when I know that there will be a dozen or twenty friends or acquaintances in either of two cafés or two, maybe three public houses, all within a few hundred yards. So many tables where I could find company, where I would not be allowed to remain alone, even if I could bring myself to remain silent. Often these pleasant encounters can be destructive. I meet a friend, and we make levellers of each other. Mutually we assume that neither of us has changed, even in mood, since last we met. We take up the conversation where we left off, two days ago, a week, a month, knowing our conditions to be so stable, conducted with such decorous economy, that we didn't even make a joke of it. We behave as if the interim had never existed; but always our exchanges progress through a perceptible and continuous time whose authority is not to be betrayed by gaps, lacunae of ignorance or incomprehension. To any question that is put tactfully enough there will be an answer. This shrinkage and acceleration of life is more painful in such a circle than it is with the people I work with, as familiar and as close to me and as time-bound as my clothes or possessions.

As I have learned to avoid it, I have come to feel that there are two cities, one in which I am documented, traceable, involved and by which I am possessed, and another in which I am merely suspended. A city for my mouth, and a city for my eye. The first I could not begin to describe, for it is by nature fluid, comfortable, made of expendable things, where anecdotes and memories harden only very slowly into myth. And myth is not welcome in it. It hounds down lies about itself so that its conscience may be free. It is very intelligent. The other city is precarious in the understanding. It occurs when the other clears away from it and leaves it bare.

I first recognised it unmistakably in a small bar one Sunday night. It was November, and it had been raining all day. Late in the afternoon a blustery wind had begun to move the clouds more rapidly, and by nightfall the rain had stopped. The night came in very close around the house, with the wind battering darkness against the windows, through which I could see lights, burning brilliant and hard, exposed and obscured variably by the swaying of branches in the gardens and the playing field beyond. And even those which shone steadily seemed across the distance to be stripped of their foggy glass. The curtain of damp had gone. I went out along the wet roadway in a palpably dry air, with the black wind blowing strongly from the west.

I got in an almost empty bus going into the city and sat at the front. It was like being on a country train very late at night, a dull, feebly lit interior trundling slowly along through a sea of intense darkness. Through the window before me stretched an unpeopled world. Hardly any other vehicles. The street lamps showing separately and precisely on their invisible standards down the long incline ahead; a few shaded windows only among the rows of bulky houses whose shapes merged into those of the swaying poplars and, with them, into the huge shapelessness of the sky; the rainy sheen of the roadway drying off to a faint matt lustre, the hissing of the tyres still just audible.

In the town, Sunday lights, just a few, and the wind lessened among the long cliffs of buildings, free to be dark, with their cornices hardly showing against the sky. People walking fast. Up the hill, round the little square with the fountain the buildings stood square-faced over the narrower streets, looking like pieces of furniture in a store, lit only by oblique street-radiance from below. Here there were fewer people: small groups scattering from the bus stops behind the museum, and one or two wanderers, going slowly nowhere. This was a place with no bright shop windows, and all of their faces, illuminated only by the pale bluish-green mercury-vapour lamps, look as though rendered faintly phosphorescent by the wind against which they walked.

Across two streets, and there was nobody at all. Past the imposing front of the long grey block of the Civic offices, and round its shadowy, undecorated back, tiled white like a lavatory. A deserted car park at the entrance to a bleak, curving street; Prospect. Again, this is a stone ghost. They planned it as a huge sweep of elegant houses looking outward over falling land. After the street had been laid out and no more than a quarter of the row built, the scheme collapsed, and the space was filled with little factories that still work on, incredibly derelict. Much of the outer side of the curve is occupied by a low wall, good to lean on. That night I stayed by it, staring across the fifty-foot drop on the other side of it and across the tarred roofs of the canal wharves below to the nearest masses of light. They were a good way away; a pond of blackness clung close around this side of the town's centre, stretching away to left and right, and a mile across. Dim shapes of roofs, some of them very large, and of chimney stacks showed above it against the vague fuzz of the light that hung over the suburbs further out. Here was a patch of the town that was almost uninhabited at this hour, a maze of factories and workshops in backyards, houses deserted by their owners, the master-men, and given over entirely to manufacture. That fight was a century ago. In the steep-sided channels of those streets there were gas lamps, but none of their light rose above the roofs. Across that dark lake was the small low upstairs workshop to which my father had gone daily for fifty years.

To the right, standing out into the blackness like a pier, I could see the Telephone exchange, humming with still white light; above its roof the television mast reared its silver-grey girders up to a blind saurian head, picked out with warning lights for the sky. The lines of buildings behind me were impassive; close as I was to the main streets, I could hardly hear the traffic. The city was carrying with it this dead weight of dark, in which nothing was growing, no words were being uttered, no lamps adding to the patterns of light. I thought of that poem of Laforgue's in which the Earth has died and the stars, a procession of magnificent suns, spin slowly in its funeral; it was as if the city, a moving nebula trailing systems of lights, bore within itself inescapably a great extinct organism, perceptible only as a densely opaque mass, hostile to light.

Yet some people lived here. In the row of sheds that lined the wharf road, right below me, there was still a pair of cottages, skulking and drab, with a street lamp head level with their curtained bedroom windows. Old people? It should have been possible for them to move; they were hardly likely to be the sort of people who would regard it as in any way piquant or smart to live in such a place. Relics. When they died, the houses would stand empty.

I went on, round to the other end of the prospect and back among the shops and the public buildings. Screened from me only by a row or two of concrete puzzle-boxes, the extinguished district I had been staring at was still sliding alongside my path, like a gulf in the mind. I would not go back that night; I knew well enough there was nothing worth dredging for among those piled workshops and alleys. I had been there often enough in daylight, and I knew more than merely the street frontages: I had had occasion to penetrate the littered yards, climb dusty unlit wooden staircases, tap on ramshackle sliding panels and wait in offices that were converted attics; there were many strange facts there, but no mystery. Yet I was obsessed with the idea that in such darkness there must be something ancient, glittering and malign that I had to plunge and grope for to show myself that I lived. The gulf reached up over the rooftops into the night sky, islanding more perfectly the few stars that showed, ancient and hateful. I was on the brink of a hopeful dream from which I could only wake too early into aridity, and I would not enter it.

I went into a large cafeteria, full of people I could not remember having seen before. Mostly homeless, mostly men, from the Rowton House or the Salvation Army, sitting with their caps on by the shiny tables, their long drab overcoats trailing on the floor. The breath from the kitchens was stale, the breath of old age, sharp with existence. All this year too familiar; if I stayed I would subside into the times I had gone there before and seen the same things, the old electric clock over the serving-hatch would start to race.

Going down the street I felt myself too close to my friends. A few paces and I would be through the door and face to face with them. Instead, I took a turning and went into the first bar I came to. I had passed it countless times: small, old-fashioned and probably cosy, with a great weight of ornate masonry heaped above it – the sort of place businessmen went at midday, scenting in its age and dowdiness a sort of practical, Dickensian conviviality, a house of character.

Whatever character they saw in it was their own, for the place was simply run down. Had the manager put any effort into it, it would have turned inevitably into a stupidly smart city pub, blinking brightly at the climbers who would frequent it. But the fittings were old, the floor bare, the shelves carelessly kept. The two barmen wore grubby white coats and cheap ties; one was a big black-haired man in his thirties, with round expressive eyes and a handsome, reddish face that was starting to sag with too much listening. He handled glasses and bottles as if he was washing up at home, without conscience or flair. He leaned on the bar and talked. The other was younger, slighter and straight-faced, with hair brushed carefully upwards. He hung back, laughing softly at his companion's backchat and showing long teeth. His head moved rather abruptly on a lean neck when he glanced, as he did frequently, towards the door.

There were only four customers: two women with fat behinds who sat at the bar on the bare wooden stools drinking Guinness, a sailor, and a little man of middle age with a belted overcoat and a surprised potato-face. The women might, from their eyes and appearance, have been the wives of the barmen, but were obviously on their way somewhere; the sailor had just come in from somewhere and the other man looked to be a fixture. All of them appeared to know the barmen, and there was a conversation that staggered along in bursts.

It was like sitting in a draughty bedroom listening to someone coughing in a nearby room, to kettles being filled, cups washed, cisterns flushed. This halting epic of their conversation was in a language with which I had thought myself familiar enough. Tonight it came confusedly across the trench of darkness I had taken in, sounding foreign. It seemed to come not so much from a foreign place as from a foreign time, a time that was not whatever it was I understood as the Present. This was the city talking, blearily and out of the back of its head, or out of its belly. One of the women put a hand inside her skirt and scratched the underside of her thigh, her smooth face with its ginger eyebrows still inclined, listening to her companion. That was the place that was speaking; that and the big barman's splayed hand, the other's interior smile, the burst of greased curls that broke from the sailor's tilted cap, the little man's lumpy cheeks and his collar, fastened under the tie-knot with a gilt pin. A language which spent itself in the effort of becoming, jetting out thickly and falling back. The only language that men could use without distorting it. If I could learn it, I would be the one who could distort it. But I had no wish to begin.

So close to the system which considered that I belonged to it, and whose commands I had to obey, I had come upon a different system, tangled with it but independent, like lymph and blood. I realised that these people were doing nothing, passing the time of night, idly rubbing the incipient crisis of their lives off against one another; that they were as bored by this circle as I would have been in my own round the corner. I knew that I was getting more pleasure from them than they were getting from themselves, but their private evaluations, the answers they would give if tactfully questioned over the months of exchanged confidences, did not concern me at that moment. After a few glances of curiosity when I first went in, bought my beer and sat back against the wall with my overcoat still buttoned up, they had paid me no attention. They must each have decided something about me, to suit themselves; but they, and the place we were in, were forced to carry me with them as the city was forced to carry that dead, deserted bowl of darkness in its coils of light. I was there but I was alien.

I could have given account of where I was, whom I saw and what I heard, using the evidence of my life; but that evidence seemed strangely distant. In becoming the black gulf of thought I had extinguished myself to Life and saw through the eye of the dead, or of inorganic matter. I saw a life without myself. In a way and for a moment it was frightening, like reading a deed of transfer which takes your own death for granted and treats you perfunctorily as an absence; then it became somnolent and clear. In that room, the world had spread effortlessly into the spaces left by the removal of my living self and had taken all the things in which I had complemented and balanced what I found there into myself. Had I, on entering, made any gesture of belonging, of sharing the moment as a living being, I should I suppose, have been given parts to play, those parts which they sketched privately in their glances at me. I should have been the learned man, the shy man, the deprecator of self, the acid humourist, the curate in mufti with the slyly bawdy mind. Take me away again and the roles would have to be redistributed among the survivors.

Detached, I saw the whole of myself added to, shared among, these people and this room. I saw a life without myself: a world into which I had not yet been born. I recalled the world as I first knew it, when I had been born only comparatively recently, and I saw similarities. Sex in the walls, from corner to corner, and without a name. Death in the ceiling and the floor, without a name. Two powers that, nameless, were simply Power, lugging these great speaking bodies to and fro, more or less elegantly, in an automatism disguised by the incomprehensible commentaries of their lips. I saw with the mystified senses of those I watched. The picture had no composition, no single dominant point of demand. The focus was multiple, and added to itself continually, with every movement, every word that made itself visible, every small jet of energy. When there was silence, grains of light scratched their way down a glass sky. The room was a limbo in dusty air, established fortuitously among the gigantic floor joists of the single building that was the city.

I left soon, not wishing to see and hear so much that I would understand the scene on its own terms. Inadvertently I had taken in too many facts, made guesses and explanations, started to tell myself stories that tempted me to find out a truth to check them against. I went there once again, but I saw at once that the place and I could not be strangers to each other. The barman, I felt, thought he knew me; we were committed to sizing each other up. I left quickly, and shall not return for a long while.

Since that time, I have sought out places where I cannot easily understand, cannot be understood. Cafés mostly; a few public houses, open spaces with seats, where people come to read the papers and feed the birds. Or parts of the city where there are few people; streets unpopulated by day, where both men and women are out at work; the factory districts that are deserted after five in the evening; the streets under the viaducts, whose long stretches of blank wall offer no invitations. Mostly, though, I prefer the cafés, and the irregularly-shaped churchyard of the baroque church in the town centre with its straight paved walks lined with planes and conical holly-bushes. I can go only rarely to the smaller cafés, for I am treated as a familiar if I go too often; I have to be affable, and the establishment begins to alter itself a little to accommodate me. In the larger ones, the cafeterias, the business is so automatic, the number of people so great, that I run no risks.

In these places, in these people, I have begun to see the body of the city, a body without a face, without a voice. I see its remoter nerves shiver and move in obedience to impulses that are out of sight in distant rows of houses, carrying messages that will for the most part fade into inertia before they reach its sluggish and ignorant roof-brain. I think the city has, indeed, no face except that which the journalists, the Press Relations Officers and the politicians paint on to it when it seems necessary; no articulate voice, only the continuous surf of sound that muffles it, the clatter of sounds that tear it surreptitiously under the surf. It has a body; a dry throat and a singing throat, a belly and a navel, armpits, elbows, privates. These are not places but moments.

23.

I have come to be able to recognise a good many men and women, mostly solitary and middle-aged or old. Again and again they come to the cafés and the public places. Some of them spend all day in the centre of the town. At first sight they seem merely lonely, looking for company, for sexual adventure maybe, even in poverty and old age.

But that loneliness is only a necessary product of their condition, and they do not seek to cure it. Their eyes are averted, their glances secretive or dull; sometimes they will talk to waitresses or policemen, but never to one another. They are people who have never been claimed. I suppose most of them have been drawn into marriages or lifetimes of work, but nothing in their lives has ever folded them into itself irrevocably. They are still looking for the world; and they come regularly to these few arenas in the heart of the city, to these extreme markets of the self where, if they can stay long enough, they will find the world in their own withering out of life, the increasing concentration on the leverage of a stiff limb, the observance of a habit, the quality and hue of a particular breath.

The persistent ones among them are few – maybe a couple of dozen. Others are cast into the habit temporarily by bereavement or cruelty or despair. Soon they go home again, or marry, or are glad to go to the Old People's Homes. They are more ready to talk. I think they rarely see fantasies, or if they do, are so afraid that they dismiss them.

There are elderly men, respectable and warmly dressed, though seedy, whom I have seen for years working patiently in the library: fantasies of scholarship. There are the older prostitutes who sit for hours in the dim bars of the Crown, through habit, quietly dressed, gossiping together or sitting alone starring peacefully in front of them, so intent and sufficient that men find it difficult to attract their attention; often they go home dazedly at closing time without trying to pick anyone up.

All of these people live so slowly and so regularly that they are to me like the stones of a familiar garden path. The days move around them rapidly and are gone, full of people bound on quick adventures but to them the passage of time is important only in respect of the weather it brings, the messages it gives to the body: and in their presence I sense in myself an unfamiliar constancy. They move in a shifting pattern in which I never see a beauty that draws me or an ugliness that repels. A heap of hard cinders that nobody moves.

24.

One Saturday at midday in the Crown the bar was crowded with paid-off builders, men on their way to football matches, and perhaps twenty women. It is a large poorly-lit, mean room in an old hotel. The walls are solidly panelled in dark wood, and the bar itself is heavily built, with bulbous carvings and shelves backed by patterned mirrors. But the wall seats are worn, the long horse hair cushions broken and uncomfortable, the linoleum on the floor has lost all its colour and taken on the lines of the boards beneath, and the chairs and tables are rickety affairs with spindly legs and round seats and tops. The women, of all ages, sat dowdily around the walls; some already had men, and the rest would get somebody at turning-out time. It was that sort of day. The place was happy. They called across to one another, and a few groups began to sing, different songs at once, which they never seemed to finish. At half-past-two the room emptied slowly, with little swirls of intrigue and a good deal of shouting. A police inspector and a sergeant came and stood at the door and then strolled through, looking about them without expression.

As usual, there was a straggling line of men outside the

clothiers across the road from the entrance, watching the women come out and make towards the bus stops, followed by little files of men, stepping out hastily and intent, some of them falling away soon to look in the shop windows. The last of the women to leave was not at first followed. I had noticed her earlier, for she was a stranger, a little mousey woman, pale with sharp eyes and nose and a small slit mouth. Her skin was papery and mottled, translucent under drab, whitish powder, and she wore grotesque clothes: a dark blue coat, pinched in tightly to a high waist, and worn over a cheap jumper; a little white hat like a pared-down sunbonnet, that obscured most of her hair; fancy white lace gloves, thick wrinkled stockings and large white shoes that looked like plimsolls. Sitting alone, wizened over a glass of stout, she had looked like one of the little drunken old ladies from the cheap wine bar nearby, or one of those who came with shopping bags full of crusts for the pigeons in the churchyard. She had come to the Crown, though, to try her luck and as she came out she looked worried and angry. She went off down the street in her white pumps. A tiny bird-like figure making long bouncing erratic strides, and looking at nobody.

A man standing in a doorway some way down watched her coming. A quiet man of about forty in a loose raincoat, with glasses and untidy straight hair. His expression was difficult to read, for his face was seriously malformed, bearing the signs of early disease or injury at birth. The lower jaw protruded lopsidedly, with the teeth resting on the upper lips; under a bulging forehead the nose was depressed, and the eyes, set wide apart lay almost on the surface of his face, protuberant and starring out of line. As the woman passed him, he turned his head to follow her, jerking himself out to catch her attention, but she did not see him. Flushing, he set out to follow. His gait in pursuit was horrible. His feet were twisted inwards, one in front of the other, and he had to move his weight forward by thrusting movements of his dangling hands, as if he was used to walking with two sticks. The woman's progress was hindered by the crowd, and she narrowed herself, slowing down to look for openings to slide through, her heavy white handbag swinging against the passers-by. At the same time he threw himself forward recklessly, risking falls, red in the face. There came a stretch when she must have been able to see him out of the corner of her eye, as he slouched almost at her shoulder, but he could not draw level.

Finally she reached the end of the street and stopped at the kerb, just as the traffic lights turned red. He halted, still just behind her, with a look of confused fright, then sidled a few yards along the pavement and looked at her, poised as she was on the edge. She turned to glance at him, thin-lipped, then sharply turned her head the other way, with set face. He backed onto the pavement again and shuffled towards her, desperately. As he reached her, she stepped into the gutter and stood there, though the traffic was hurtling past inches away. He leaned his frightful face over her shoulder and said something; she jerked away, and shut her eyes, while he stood still with his head tilted back, gazing down his face at her little hat beneath him. The lights changed, and she strode out while the last cars were still moving past, clutching her bag in both hands. The waiting crowd poured past him, hiding her from sight. He stood immobile on the curb, stricken and blank, then turned and dragged himself back up the street. A cow-eyed policewoman, blond and handsome, stood by the wall, her black-gloved hands behind her back. She watched him calmly as he went.

25.

The city asleep. In it there are shadows that are sulphurous, like tanks of black bile. The glitter on the roadways is the deceptive ore that shines on coal.

The last buses have left the centre: the pallid faces of the crowd looked like seed-pods, filled by a sick and gusty summer that had come too late for plenty.

Silvered rails that guide pedestrians at street corners stand useless. Towards midnight, or at whatever hour the sky descends with its full iron weight, the ceilings drop lower everywhere; each light so partial, and proper only to its place. There is no longer any general light, only particular lights that overlap.

Out of the swarming thoroughfares, the night makes its own streets with a rake that drags persuaded people out of its way; streets where the automatic signals go on repeating themselves wisely through the hours of darkness, and where the greater buildings have already swung themselves round to odd angles against the weakened currents of the traffic.

There are lamp lit streets where the full darkness is only in the deep drains and in the closed eye sockets and shut throats of the old as they lie asleep; their breath moves red tunnel-lights in their nostrils.

The artificial highways hold their white-green lights with difficulty, like long loaded boughs; when the machines stop moving down them, their gradients reappear.

Journeys at night, sometimes grooves in a thick substance, sometimes raised weals on a black skin.

The city at night has no eye, any more than it has by day, although you would expect to find one; and over much of it, the sleep is aqueous and incomplete, like that of a hospital ward.

But to some extent it stops, drops and congeals. It could be broken like asphalt; and the men and women rolled out like sleeping maggots.

26.

A gospeller in the market at midday, standing hemmed in by his hearers. At his back, the spiked green railings of a public lavatory, a telephone box, a shuttered newspaper kiosk. He is a little man with bushy brows, long grey hair and a fine nose in a flushed face; his big knobbly hands are clasped in front of him, clutching a worn shopping bag. He wears a raincoat and his shoes are broken. With his eyes almost closed he shouts hoarsely against the traffic, fights back at the hecklers with a sorrowful good humour that he preserves with difficulty.

Two of these stand close beside him, facing the crowd as if part of his act. They do this every day, without tiring. On his right is a little Irishwoman, pug-faced, neatly dressed with good shoes. Her eyes are pale and round, her face, under a great, girlish fringe, lined with grimaces. On his left stands a big handsome man, ruddy-faced and hot-eyed, with pouting lips and waved fair hair. He wears a short-belted waterproof and his trousers are tucked tightly into heavy gumboots. He stands proudly, sweating in the brilliant sunshine with thumbs tucked theatrically into his belt, and looks down with a gaze of fixed scorn at the speaker, who reaches no higher than his shoulder. One of his eyelids droops. The Irishwoman is hunched up into an attitude of mock devotion, her teeth inanely bared and her eyes rolled upwards. She listens intently, moaning and shivering.

The gospeller, balancing on the kerb, his feet neatly together, tries to ignore them. He cries: – 'My dear friends. I know that God has gathered you here today in your dinner time to hear His words of comfort. When you go away to your work I hope you will take with you some of His light. We know he sent his Son, Jesus Christ, to die for us and forgive us our sins –'

The big man taps him on the shoulder and winks at the crowd.

'to forgive us our sins and to make sure – and make no mistake of this, friends, – that each and every one of us who takes heed of His word shall live in everlasting glory above!'

'Here. Wait a minute.' The big man stands in front of him and addresses the crowd. 'How do we know all this?' He walked back to his place glowering and smiling by turns.

'My dear friend, we know it by this book –'. He reached in his bag and drew out a big black bible with a soft cover fastened by a button. 'This book that tells each and every one of us of God's wonderful promise through the life and death of Christ Jesus.' He opens and shuts his mouth, rubbing the book with his thumb.

The heckler mutters: the Irishwoman suddenly stands transfixed with memory, then capers round, singing.

'Some say the Devil's dead

And some say it's blarney

But some say the devil's dead

And buried in Killarney – how about that Minister? The devil's dead! Whee!'

'Oh no, oh no. The Evil One lives yet among us, in every heart. But – I tell you again – the sins he makes us do shall be forgiven–'

'I don't want my sins forgiven,' says the man. 'I enjoy 'em. You don't mean to tell me,' he thunders, menacing, 'an ordinary little bloke like you can come here and tell these people what's right? Garn.' He folds his arms and waits, his brows crooked fiercely. Some of the crowd laugh. Many of them are tame, jaded men in raincoats, solemn motherly women. But here and there are great coarse heads, maniacal and grinning: beast faces with broken teeth, blotched and swollen features. There is a line of them on the step behind the speaker: a man with a face like an ape, a mask of thick grey skin, pitted with black-heads; another with black stubble covering his long reddened face almost to the eyes and a wet twitching mouth; a little cross-eyed man wearing only a footballer's jersey under his jacket. These faces are sadistic, predatory, but simple, moulded from within by forces that have never considered concealment. Among them is a rosy faced old man in a soft brown hat who smiles about the crowd delightedly.

The preacher struggles on, beginning to gabble. He opens the bible and reads, apparently at random, from an Old Testament prophet, with the tall man shouting him down at every verse. At last he protests:

'My good friend, can't you see you are only making a fool of yourself in front of these good people? They are seriously listening to the word of God who –'

'You know bloody well they've come for a bit of fun; we're only trying to help you out. You ought to be grateful to us. Hadn't he?'

'My dear sir. My dear sir, I call to mind a man who once thought as you do. His name was Henry Wilkes and he came to God in the year 1872 in the city of Liverpool. When he was a young man he made fun of God whenever he could. Filthiness was second nature to him –'

The woman, with gestures, recites:

'Said Farmer Brown as he wiped his eye,

It's praise be to God that cows don't fly!'

She titters and curtsies, applauding herself.

' – One moment. One moment. He drank heavily. He went with the worst sort of women.'

'Oh hark at him, the dirty old man,' she cries roguish, 'he's been convertin' 'em down in the kips. Been at the mols have you, darling.' She listens again, her eyes closed. The big man grins round, screwing a finger into his temple.

The preacher starts again and goes on talking, faster and faster. After a moment of listening the woman flings her legs wide apart and leans back, shouting at the top of her voice:

'O the lying dirty smelly bleeders there! O the sin and shame of it inside!'

She sets her hands on her hips and thrusts her stomach out clumsily jerking it obscenely back and forth. 'I stay out all day because I'm scared of the dirty lying sneaking filth! Do I make myself clear? Do I make myself clear?'

She opens her eyes wide and shrinks back to the edge of the crowd, glancing worriedly about and clicking her tongue.

'Thank you all for listening, ladies and gentlemen. God bless you. Goodbye. God bless you.' He thrusts his way through the crowd behind him, and the benign old gentleman in the brown hat steps quickly forward and begins to speak, slowly and quietly.

'Now friends, my colleague has spoken some wonderful things to you. Before we part I should like to introduce to you another great friend of mine...'

A lean young man in American clothes makes his way through the crowd easily, nodding and smiling, keen eyed and serious. His hair is cropped short and his jaw truculent. He draws from a briefcase a sheaf of printed papers. The crowd begins to disperse.

27.

In an afternoon of dazzling sunlight in the thronged streets, I saw at first no individuals but a composite monster, its unfeeling surfaces matted with brick-dust: a mass of neck, limbs without extremities, trunks without heads; unformed stirrings and shovings spilling across the streets it had managed to get itself provided with.

Later, as the air cooled, flowing loosely about the buildings that stood starkly among the declining rays, the creature began to divide and multiply. At crossings I could see people made of straws, rags, cartons, the stuffing of burst cushions, kitchen refuse. Outside the Grand Hotel, a long-boned, carrot-haired girl with glasses loping along, with strips of bright colour, rich, silky green and blue, in her soft clothes. For a person made of such scraps she was beautiful.

Faint blue light dropping down through the sparse leaves of the plane trees in the churchyard opposite after sundown, cooling and shaping heads, awakening eyes.

28.

The Giantess in the suburbs. In the district where I was born, and from which for many years I hardly ever travelled, there were, and still are, a few women of great size and self-possession, who stride about the shops like proud aboriginal survivors. They do not dress like the housewives of the district; they are seen rarely, mostly in fair weather, and never with men or with children. Their size makes them smooth and calm.

One is the statue of a mother. Full bosomed and broad hipped, she walks with neat clicking feet along the pavements in summer in a crisp light suit, her elbows out a little and her head, with its grey hair parted in the middle and curved into a bun, carried high, she glances about her with a pleasant look, but greets nobody. She has a dry skin, with a high, arrogant colour, and a solid, composed face, almost that of a man.

Another is younger, heavily athletic, and deep tanned, with coarse black hair that falls in long waves over a powerful neck. She's over six feet tall. Her figure is good, and she dresses like a certain sort of actress, in a tight dark-blue summer dress, and sunglasses that emphasis the strong brows, the high narrow brow, the hooked nose, and the full, painted mouth. She walks like an actress, from the hips, precisely, in high heels, in such a way that, were she less extravagantly built, she would attract too much attention. But her effect is raw, the lines so spacious that the textures of the rough dress, the dark-downed forearms, the round expanse of brown shoulder, spring out and tear disturbingly across the formal idea of woman; and her eyes when they can be seen, are, though vague and sensitive, huge like those of an animal.

There are four or five others like these two, seen less frequently. Once I met such a woman face to face, but she behaved out of character. I had been playing the piano in a three-piece band at a Saturday night dance. It was in a large ugly old suburban public house on a main road; the upstairs room was long, narrow and high, with a brightly lit bar at one end and a shadowy little dais for the musicians at the other. The band had been hurriedly assembled: none of us three had met either of the others before, and our music was appalling. No more than fifteen people had come in during the whole evening, and most of them had left long before it finished.

At half-past-eleven, we packed the instruments away and put on our overcoats over our dinner-jackets. As I was closing the piano lid, she came tripping across the dance floor, surprisingly lightly, from the little group of the landlord's friends who were still chatting with him and singing down by the bar. She was very beautiful. About forty, with dark hair and a perfectly clear skin, a broad face with regular features and fine, light-coloured eyes set wide apart. She was extremely tall, and although full-bodied, strapping even, was not fat. She wore a neat navy-blue suit, and a simple blouse of white silk, and although she was a little drunk, she still balanced on her head an enormous flat white disc of a hat, like a tier of a wedding cake. She ogled the three of us with her big eyes.

'Boys, can you play us the Welsh National Anthem?' she asked, appealingly, in a high, musical Swansea voice.

The others muttered and guffawed to themselves. Straight-faced, I sat down and played 'Land of My Fathers', *maestoso*, by guesswork, with feeling and a few mistakes.

'Bravo!' she cried, clapping. 'He knows it! Play it again, love.' And she ran off, gaily on smooth legs.

A few minutes later, I was standing beside the group by the bar, with the others, trying to look purposeful. Nobody had shown any sign either of wishing us good night or paying us. After a while the landlord took the saxophone player aside and started to hesitate over a wad of pound notes, counting them off with a wetted thumb. Exhausted, I stood watching. I was morbidly disgusted, and I must have looked very miserable. She saw me, and opening her eyes wide, left the sagging little man she was talking to.

'Oh, didn't he play lovely?' she cried. 'Didn't you? Played one for me.'

I smiled, sourly I suppose, for she cocked her head on one side and stood regarding me with what looked like astonishment from a yard away. Her scent reached me, fresh and in a way antiseptic.

'Don't you talk?' she said bemusedly.

Apologetically, I yawned, to show how tired I was. She giggled, and stepping forward popped a forefinger into my mouth just before it closed. We stood there for some seconds, I stupefied, but with a sudden cold sensation at the back of my head, she with her finger in my mouth and an expression of gay delight on her face. I closed my teeth gently on the finger.

'Ow!' she said. 'Ooh!' Then a trill of laughter. She pulled the finger. I held it. Her arm was crooked elegantly. She rested her chin on the raised wrist and the world turned into her great clear face, shadowed by the spreading hat. She rested the tip of her nose on the tip of mine and using it as a pivot, began to rock her head slowly from side to side, fixing me with her eyes until I grew dizzy, and tugging steadily at the finger. I let it go, rather suddenly and she reeled away, walking backwards until she reached her little man, who appeared not to have been watching. She stood pouting across at me, flapping her hand before the man's apparently sightless eyes.

'Oh, he bit me,' she complained. 'He's a biter. See if it's bleeding.' With an effort, the man stared at me, then coughed loudly. I wondered whether it would be better to retreat or risk a quarrel; but he lost interest, and started fumbling in his pocket for cigarettes.

A little while later, we were standing across the road at the bus stop, with half an hour to wait. The two of them came out. He had a hat on and was walking quickly; she had a hand tucked under his armpit and was talking continuously. Rapidly they passed along the front of the darkened building and suddenly vanished into the black entrance of its car park. No car came out. There was no sound of an engine. Twenty minutes passed.

Then they came out again. Her arm was round his shoulders, his round her waist. They walked as quickly as before along the front of the public house and disappeared round the corner of the street, conversing earnestly.

I admire the Giantess. Exiled by her physique from the concealment, the retreat, the anonymous, deadly mother-hood into which most women eagerly pass, she has nevertheless not allowed her body to fall away, broken-footed, and obesely dragging in the hope of reaching a pathetic inertia at floor level. She has to live with pre-carious vigilance. If she lies passive she will be attacked by vermin.

29.

There are ashes that belong to other people. Propped up on the shelves of the bar where the dance was held were two framed pictures, black-and-white caricatures of the publican and his wife. They were done in a style that was popular in newspapers thirty or forty years ago, with huge heads ballooning from tiny spruce bodies, dressed in flat black with pointed, shiny feet. The portraits were merciless, exaggerating his baldness, her crimped hair, the fulsomely grinning dentures of both. This was how they were pleased to imagine themselves.

30.

Of these people I now see so regularly in the town, those who have fallen off from the belly of England to starve, living off their own bodies, the men seem stunned and quiet, trying to be still. The older women, too, are placid, their energy almost gone. I see flagrant eccentricity only in three or four of the women, all of them in early middle-age.

I have seen the little Irishwoman again. She stands by the building sites shouting cheerfully up at the workmen, then swearing. She sits in cafés muttering to herself and casting suspicious glances until people move away, leaving her isolated in a ring of tables and chairs. She is far gone; soon she will be locked away, among rooms and bodies that will increase her terror. She will become a shrunken, still body, rapidly aging, containing a cold, voluble intelligence that splits progressively into fragments under the strains of its circling motion.

There are three others, who might be sisters, walking near one another in separate solitudes. They look haggard and lonely, simplified to a linear monotony by their lack of reactions to the world – and hence beautiful. Yet when the world, attracted, moves toward them at all, they start and snarl in distrust; they withdraw and quickly forget.

The moment of the city where they are most themselves is the Roman one: the western edge of the centre in the late afternoon of a clear day in late autumn or early spring. A high, cold, Palladian sky, the sun setting behind the ridges of the Town Hall, and armed statues poised under the starlings' flight behind the low stone cornices. At that hour they come from their work and take Tea in the cafés, staying sometimes for hours, going from one to another, until they are roofed in with darkness and begin, sullenly, to shine.

One is a slender graceful woman with the face of a bird; fine arched brows and quick eyes under drooping lids. She dresses expressively but quietly, sometimes in a cape. She wears a nonchalant smile, tosses her head as she walks, as if secretly pleased and strikes elegant poses, gloved hand on hip, as she pauses to gaze in shop windows with well-bred indifference. Her movement is sinuous to the point of being provocative; but it is apparent that the sinuous body moves by defensive habit, independently of the dreaming head, whose toss does not quite conceal an almost continuous tense quiver.

Her meal is ritualistic. She chooses a seat with care, in a withdrawn corner, and lays her gloves, handbag and book in a three-sided palisade about her place, with sugar, pepper and salt clustering about it. Then, with a backward glance at the management, she goes to the self-service counter and collects her food. A salad, a buttered bun, a cup of coffee. She eats slowly, and with delicate absorption, her gaze moving continually over her possessions, with solicitous pleasure, like that of an amateur shepherdess over her toy flock. When she looks up, it is with eyes still veiled in concentration, gazing kindly but loftily at the surroundings without expecting to see anything of interest. Her hand quivers, her eyes dart here and there, but except when she is eating, her mouth never moves from its faint, tolerant smile.

The second woman is tall, with thick white skin, sensually built, yet eyeless, evasive, cold as a snowdrift; a handsome comfortable body, deep and still like a coffin, wrapped always in soft black; a big loose coat that swings easily about her heavy limbs, a shapeless velvet hat that falls from a band set high over the thick, springing wintery-blonde hair to counter the hard and icy lines of the deserted face. Her ways are most regular. Every evening at the same hour she comes to the big, cheap cafeteria and sits under the harsh lights, eating a large meal, reading the evening paper and smoking a cigarette. Then she crosses the town, always by the same devious route through darkened side-streets, and catches the same bus. The moments when I see her show no variation, no story. They are a single moment that adds to itself and becomes older, deeper, more luminous.

Only her movements about the café are unpredictable. She gets each course of her meal from the counter separately and, abandoning the used dishes, moves to another seat, maybe at the other end of the room. Altogether she might move five or six times in the course of her hour, choosing her places without appearing to deliberate, but behaving on each occasion as if she had just entered from the street. She pays no attention to anyone; I have never properly seen her eyes. Her pale head bowed over her plate, she eats almost brutishly, gripping the knife and fork in her ringed hands.

Her clothes are too fine for the place, chosen with style and with an obvious knowledge of her own appearance. Her face is of a kind rarely seen among the undistinguished and distorted features of the others who go there. It must always have been a severe face: a calm forehead, wrinkled across when the strong, angular brows are raised; the eyes underlined and set beneath hooded lids, subtly painted; a straight nose, snubbed at the tip and sensitive, with wide nostrils. The cheekbones are prominent and the line of the jaw square and firm. The lips are long and full, curving with some disdain in the vague white face, and pursed between two deep lines of strain, that sometimes twist the corners of her mouth upwards in a creased, mask-like grin that has no humour in it.

If her eyes were predatory and alive she would look like a whore whose stock-in-trade was the theatrical and stately, for her face is painted for a coarse immediate effect in dim artificial light. The glare of the cafeteria, attacking from all angles, is too much for it, showing the marks of the effort she must make to prevent her still expression from disintegrating. Occasionally, when the grin fails to relieve the strain, a cheek, the tip of the nose, one eye, the forehead, will twitch rapidly.

She walks abruptly, with a rapid, feminine swing of one arm, and a handbag tucked firmly under the other, her head held down as if against a wind, and thrust slightly forward. She always seems to know where she is going;

she never looks more than cursorily at the traffic or the people who might block her way, moving, I suppose, with an automatic intelligence that leaves her free with whatever it is that detains her mind.

I first saw the third woman late one night, stalking under the lamps in the churchyard in a fur coat, stopping to stare down a walk then turning and parading back, as if in a travesty of the similar but more surreptitious activities of the street-women who occasionally came there. She was a lean woman with short straggly hair dyed red, the dye growing out and giving way to streaks of grey. As she stood under a lamp, with her hands in the pockets of her coat, hugging it about her, she looked away into the distance with brilliant, alarmed eyes, searching. The light showed a goose face with pouches of long resignation and dismay, and a scrawny neck with soft folds of skin. She looked like an abandoned teacher or secretary. An arrogance in the ragged head, neat ankles. She could still call a taxi, and sweep her skirts into it deftly.

Now she appears sometimes suddenly in the streets, at once peremptory and startled, as though she had just swooped down from a rooftop, like a starling. She will jerk into a café and sit there with a rolled exercise book and a packet of cheap cigarettes before her. She never eats, sometimes buys nothing at all. She stares perpetually into nothing, never shifting her gaze. The brilliant eyes are slightly bloodshot.

Unlike the other two, who appear more than ordinarily robust, she has a body so eaten up and degraded by nervousness that she appears to have no sex left. Her excitement is one of fear, that is not round or shiny or quick but constant and dragging.

I can tell what it is like for a man who is deranged to go out into the town, light-headed and obsessed, coming apart, sagging over the tubular railings of the bus shelter, finding that one leg is walking obstinately along the opposite side of the street. His fear is of what he will do; whether he will cut the rind of the world and feel its gashed lips engulf him in bitterness, or whether the rain of vengeance will strike haphazardly at his discreet selves from doorways, roofs, trees, times, eyes, fists, directions.

He will not behave sexually: his actions will merely be a gawky travesty of the phallic; a jerky walk, stiff limbs, angular glances, collapses, huddlings and swearings. He extends, and is received, taken from himself; disappears into his several pains. He is taken not by those who have waited to prey upon him but by those who agree to tolerate him. What they do with him has nothing to do with his maleness, just as the guise in which he appears is a denial of the sexual standard.

A woman who feels herself to be going mad will also attempt to make herself normal, undistinguished, tolerable. But the most acceptable woman is bound to be an object of sexual regard, even if she does nothing, and what she thinks of as pleasant when preparing herself, will prove attractive to some men. The unbalanced woman will carefully, elegantly, lock up pleasure in herself, with no intention of release, for she needs it. She will produce, by exaggeration, the suggestive. And, in part, she will know it. She will dress 'as a woman' because she is afraid of being recognised as the child or animal or bunch of flowers or birdcage she really is; and she will fear the effect she makes 'as a woman' because she is mortally afraid of sexual intrusion.

I have seen men make overtures to such women, believing the very awkwardness of their coquetry to reveal desire. If it does reveal desire, it is not a desire for the sexual act, but for the stable existence of childhood.

When I first noticed these three, I thought I was seeing in each of them a walk upwards into a personal tragedy; dramas that were being brought before the city. Now I have come to recognise their resilience, their constancy and endurance. The upward thrusts in their lives, the forces that drove them into solitude and the public places, are in the past – perhaps far in the past. They are like briars that loop along the top of a hedge, or overhead. They will not rise higher.

31.

I have begun to see the city, and my life in it, only in the last few months. Every so often now, while I'm walking along, or reading, I feel a jerk, a grating contact with something firm. This is electrifying. It is happening in the places I have inhabited for years; yet now the story is different, the models in the shop windows begin to tell the histories of their lives. At last I have been here long enough. Long enough to realise that I can bear to be alone as much of my time as I can set apart for myself. In the places to which I now go whenever I can, sometimes for an hour, sometimes for a whole afternoon and evening, I am becoming known by sight. There seems no other means of knowledge there, and for that I am grateful.

To be among other solitary people is real, reassuring, a momentary flattening of the polished curve of pure loneliness. I have known that state, towards the end of a holiday spent alone at home. In the streets, for days, all the faces have been those of strangers. I had begun to think I understood them. I had looked at them as if they were displayed for me to read or not to read, as it suited me. Then suddenly, from among all those hundreds of faces, one took into itself all the force, all the malice and destructiveness that I had forgotten. It was not looking at me, but I was afraid, knowing that when next I met it it would be I who was the victim of its disdain, its poking cruelty. One furtive sneer from it would be enough to start the general attack, the retribution of all the eyes, all the windows and streets, that I had imagined myself master of. That panic would set me off in a desperate search for contact with any friends I could find. I would perform any duties I could persuade the world to impose on me. I would hide my vulnerable self in the garments of harmless activities.

But these people who are a little mad look at me often, and incuriously. Without protest, they let me share their absence from life.

32.

He lay in bed trying to sleep. He had been there about three hours and was now resolved not to move anymore. He was relaxed, and his thoughts, that had at first been like a garish headlong journey from one lighted room to another, now drifted clean like a plane of silver mist above him in the dark. But a tingling, first in his ankles, then in his knees, made him think his posture was in some way impeding his circulation. He shifted slightly, but it made no difference, especially in his hands, like twinkling points of light that were determined, by darting about on the surface of his dark limbs, to keep him awake.

He felt himself invaded by the sensation, but managed to remain still, offering himself passively to the minute pricklings that were now moving gently over his whole body, weaving a mesh between it and the soft sheets that were above and below it. He opened his eyes and, without stirring his head, gazed about the room. It was full of a shadow that dissolved its limits and led out into corridors and recesses that did not exist. He knew that only his skin was awake.

He closed his eyes and found himself watching numberless stabs and points of light, like frost. They came and went in no pattern, so far as he could see, but some of them were more intense and durable than others. He noticed after a while that these stronger scintillations always appeared where he was least expecting them; and he set himself the task of trying to predict the area of his vision where the next one would appear, and the interval of time that separated it from the last.

When he began this he was conscious of the points of light behind his closed lids, the tingling sensations which they echoed, and a distant uniform hiss of sound, like the playing-in grooves of a gramophone record. As he concentrated on his task, and began to imagine he saw some system in the incidence of the stronger strokes of light, this sound faded, and was gradually replaced by that of voices, talking rhythmically in some inexact and syncopated relation to the movement of the lights. He seemed to be hearing them through a wall or through his pillows, and could hear nothing of what they were saying. He was too absorbed in his deliberate study of what he saw to listen;

and he was unwilling to risk starting broad awake by a switch of attention. He could not help, however, distinguishing three voices, all of them female. There seemed to be two older women talking with a young girl. For a moment, the twinkling lights became motes in a dust-filled sunbeam that came steeply through a high window; there was a pale striped wallpaper, with pink and beige in it. Then the swirling star patterns reestablished themselves. Now he could hear the voices more clear and incisive, with even an occasional word, that meant nothing to him. It was clear that the two older women were upbraiding the girl, who was responding with a desperate sullenness and shame. The girl was a daughter. Her mother, and an aunt. The mother heavy and feminine, the aunt straight and sour. The girl must have an oval face and long hands. The father was away; his voice would break too cavernously among the moving lights. A memory of the shadows of the bedroom, obscuring them, swirling about the skirts of the voices. He remembered that this room in which he lay had once been a sitting room in a vicarage. Sixty, seventy years ago. The voices grew no more distinct; the pattern of their complaint and denial, accusation and defence, continued without pause. Hearing it repeated and developed, varied and prolonged, all without a single word that would tell him what the girl had done, he fell asleep and did not dream.

33.

I find myself expecting to meet the stony woman who lay naked in the stonemason's yard. I have sensed her image in the new buildings, but she cannot be so arid and formal as they. I cannot avoid coming face to face with her soon, a live woman. She must live, though she seemed a corpse when I saw her. For a day or two, I thought she must have been a woman whose murder I read of in a newspaper; but she needs to move, as the bird and the ashes do not – must not.

I have thought of that bird again. In a café, at a slack hour of the evening. On the surface, sprawled in my seat, dully staring at a man who had just entered. Within, a vast spread, a stupendous heaviness and recessive depth, the inside of a mountain, Greek or Caucasian, ancient. A sense of indulgence towards a curious pale bird, gawky, not a good bird, that was flying there in the cavern. Standing below, on the rocky floor, an elderly man in a loose brown suit with a waistcoat, a rumpled collar and a blue tie. A man with sprouting untidy hair and a fat drooping moustache; the lower jaw unshaven but not quite bearded. He viewed the bird with hope and pride, showing his pleasure at the gradual sleeking and plumping of its feathers. Slowly, in that remote past, it was becoming the bird I know, and I grew less indulgent towards it, abandoning it to his care and to the shadows. As I first saw it, it seemed much more like the woman, warm, inept, shining for beauty. That rings true, for I think that woman I saw is a more primitive and simple image than the raven. Yet I shall understand it before I understand her.

I am quite sure I have never met her. She is not the giantess, nor any of the mad women, nor the red-haired girl I saw with Madeley. She is not any girl or woman I have known in the past, when I did not keep myself so remote.

I can have little idea of what she will look like. All I

know is that I shall have to face a woman of a certain temperament, someone who will seem strange maybe. Over the years during which I have been building those images I have so lately, so baldly discovered, I have not been advancing towards any great hope of pleasure. Though lately, the idea of the white bird as it was before it achieved form, the ghost voice of the guilty daughter coming across the borders of sleep, have made me feel that my fate may contain some freedom; these spring days I come often upon a sort of ecstasy, a rag of light blowing among the things I know, making me feel that I am not the one for whom it was intended, that I have been inadvertently looking through another's eyes and have seen what I cannot receive. And I have found it possible to move again among young people, younger often than myself. The discipline of the extreme, the solitary and the alienated is secure in me.

34. [a]

As a child, when I first learned to ride a bicycle I was not allowed to go far from home, or to cross main roads. I would go where I liked and retail, on my return, accounts of fabulous and prolonged journeys, entirely through back streets. One misty Sunday morning I found I had cycled round to the side of the town furthest from my home, a side I had never seen before. The street I was on seemed to be leading further away from home and I had to get back quickly. I knew I had to turn right but there were no side streets. A built-up hill rose steeply on that side, while to the left only a few narrows streets of old house fell away, ending obviously at the wall of a goods yard.

Ahead of me a great arch carried the railway across the road. A deep span: there must have been half a dozen or more tracks across it. Streetlamps burned under it though it was broad daylight, and water trickled down the walls and into the gutter. I stopped. I did not wish to have to go back the way I had come. I saw to my left a narrow alleyway leading downhill between tall walls, one of which that of the railway viaduct, solid-banked after its stride across the road, towered to a great height, featureless and forbidding, stretching forward as far as I could see. The alleyway was very narrow and fascinated me. But it was useless, and there was no time to explore it. I glanced across the road. From an unnoticeable opening it continued up the hill. I wheeled my bike into it and climbed; the cobbled path was too steep for riding. The alley was just wide enough for a man leading a carthorse; there were patches of trodden dung, wisps of straw, and a thin stone channel in the middle that showed, here and there, the stale of horses. I could see the long creek of pale foggy sky, far above me, and the blue rag bricks of the railway wall to my left and of another, also more than naturally high, to the right.

The alley was not perfectly straight and the roadway I had left was soon out of sight behind me; I could see several hundred yards ahead, but no end, no alteration was visible, except for what looked like the backs of station buildings above the left hand wall. On the other side I saw a recess, the size of a door. It contained a short flight of steps which appeared to open into the sky. I propped the cycle on the steps and walking up them came out into a large asphalted space like a playground, walled about and with old houses and factories visible around it.

The space was almost filled with giant plane trees, grimy and stiff, standing in the shapes of avenues among the tarmac. There were a few benches, and scattered about, some dirty battered tombstones, the heads of vaults, railed about and with willow herb growing in the cracks. I read the inscriptions on some of them. The most recent was dated somewhere about 1850. In the middle of the area was a bare rectangle big enough to hold a sizeable church, but marked only by a drain. Through the trees I could see the suburbs spread out below me to the south, but the only way out was into a street that seemed to lead back downhill, so I returned to the alley, and came out in a few minutes on a street almost in the centre of the city, beside the hoarding-masked tunnel-mouth where the railway cut into the hill. I knew where I was.

34. [b]

Easter. Alone now for three days. After two more I shall be forced to meet people. Even the owners of the house have gone away. Yesterday, Sunday, my sister telephoned to ask if I would go to the family tea; and a friend to invite me to a party that he hoped would last all night. I was affable with both, told them I was on the point of leaving town to stay [with] old friends some distance away. No one has come to visit me.

Now, at noon, I can look down from the open window of my sitting-room over the gardens where one or two of the neighbours are working. April is well advanced, and it is a light, clear day. The factories have been shut long enough for the smoke to have shifted, and the air comes in from the bright horizon, moving over the city just as it has been moving over the uneven plain to the south, with its glistening hedges and cold sunlit fields. It brushes the stark elms of the suburb that are late coming into leaf.

I want to believe I live in a single world. That is why I am keeping my eyes at home while I can. The light keeps separating the world like a table knife: it sweeps across what I see and suggests what I do not. The imaginary comes to me with as much force as the real, the remembered with as much force as the immediate. The countries on the map divide and pile up like ice-floes. What is strange is that I feel no stress, no grating discomfort among this confusion, no loss, only a belief that I should not be here. I see the iron fences and shallow ditches of the countryside the mild wind has travelled over. I cannot enter that countryside, but I cannot escape it. I cannot join the mild wind with the shallow ditches. I cannot lay April across the world and watch it slide away. Each thought is at once translucent and icily capricious. A polytheism without gods.

Last night, late, I listened to music on the radio. It was like being locked in a dark room with a window it was impossible to curtain. The will of the music seemed inane, though it was not, and became sinister by its force. The very intrusion of a form into my passivity was destructive, thrusting into my life that is made stable in these few days by dreams that presume to move forward into the day with me, sitting at breakfast, glossing the books I read.

Previously, when I have experienced such an access of dreams, I have felt unusually close to myself; this time I feel that the dreams are trying to ignore me. I have attracted them to myself only twice since I have been alone here, by a sort of pantomime, a rough joke at the expense of my public personality. On Saturday afternoon it was raining gustily and miserably. Outside, I saw awaiting me what I had stayed indoors for. I put on the most quietly perverse clothes I could find, regretted purchases or worn-out things. There was a seedy striped shirt, inherited from a dead uncle years ago; I had neither worn it, nor, for some reason, thrown it away. A pair of baggy flannels, likewise a gift. A brown pullover, discarded years ago when the elbows wore through; a pair of thick army socks and some brown shoes with pointed toes, that I had gone to dances in years ago. A tartan tie. Over all this I put on the jacket of a lounge suit, and a light overcoat I had caused to be made years ago, a fawn thing of ridiculously stylish cut, like a cavalry officer's, with slits, decorative pockets, and fancy rows of stitching at the cuffs; it had been made for half the normal price, in a cheap material that had become so rumpled and sagging in a matter of weeks that I had grown too ashamed to wear it, for it was still showy, though seedy. I remembered I had a hat somewhere: a lustrous grey waterproof trilby. This alone was enough to disguise me. I turned the brim down all the way round, and looked at myself in the mirror. An unnaturally quiet face gazed at me limply from under the hat. I was no longer myself; I had ceased altogether to be English, and was, rather, some comfortable refugee from Eastern Europe, a respectable citizen of a devastated country where clothes were shoddy and hard to come by. I am used to dressing with a certain easy monotony, a consonance of style that aims, I suppose, to unify and somehow to present in a recognisable form what I feel to be an elusive and easily divided personality. In this way, I hope people will be enabled to conjure-up a more consistent image of me than I can have of myself. Had I expected to meet anyone I knew, I would never have gone out in this assortment of garments which, by all telling different stories, combined to present me in an unfamiliar way. But I knew such a meeting would be unlikely.

In the hallstand by the door were three good walking sticks, the property of my deceased predecessor in these rooms, an elderly insurance agent. They were the only things his relatives had left after the funeral, and I had never disturbed them. Now I took one, and walked slowly off through the light rain to post a few letters.

I had about a quarter of a mile to go, along a road of large old houses, pleasantly kept, with dark trees and shrubberies half hiding them. I went leisurely, feeling the even pavement through my thick soles and the rhythmic jarring of my stick. This I felt, and the air, and the new circumstances of my dress. I saw a subdued backcloth of stylised shapes in brown, grey and silver – the empty roadway, the houses, their wet roofs, the sky – and before it, certain things that began to show distinct and wilful, like details in a work of art or the memorable and insistent elements of dreams. There were the hard, glossy cream-painted window frames of a house; the formal lines of still branches hanging over the pavement and touched with points of a raw unsoftened green; the solitary scarlet cylinder of the post-box. Listening to the music last night, I experienced once more the sensations these gave me; but where I found the music thrusting and impossible, intrusive, walking that afternoon I was able to leave these hard and assertive shapes where they stood, formally acknowledged but no more. I felt the hostility I often have towards works of art, the stubborn resistance; but I could watch the assertion and resistance idly. I let my steps become slower, until I stopped under the branches of a great larch that grew in a front garden and overshadowed the road. I stood against the low wall. The rain had not yet penetrated the boughs, and the soil of the flower-bed, which stretched away from the wall at waist-level, was dry and crumbling. A few little tufts of lobelia grew there. Where I had expected to smell damp earth and leaves, I became conscious of a strong and pervasive odour, like wet paste or distemper: the smell of a newly-built house. I scooped up a little of the soil and sniffed at it, thinking that some chemical fertiliser had been mixed with it, but there was no trace. The scent had no source that I could find, and there was no wind to be carrying it. As soon as I walked on it vanished. In this, I had reached the terminus of my outward journey, and even as I walked the last few yards to the pillar-box, I was already returning.

I stared at the windows of the nearer houses. I noticed one, curtained elegantly in yellow, with an ornately shaded standard lamp set in the bay. In the darkness of the room I could see the bluish flicker of a television screen, and as I passed I met the gaze of an anomalous middle-aged woman who was sitting alone on a high sofa before the set, but with her head turned towards the window. Her hair was dyed a dark reddish colour and curled; she wore what looked like a silk suit, pale blue and smartly cut. Her chin propped on her hand, she stared out with an expression of profound discontent which, as her stony little eyes followed me, was neither intensified nor dispelled.

Yesterday, at the same hour, I repeated the excursion similarly dressed, but varying my dandyism by a spotted bow-tie. The rain was a faint, gusty drizzle, somewhat colder, and the landscape more defined. I could not be sure whether the plastery scent still hung under the larch, or whether I willed it there again. But nothing disturbed me. When I came near the yellow-curtained window I could see that the television set was again switched on, and I looked for the solitary woman. She was not there. Instead, seated side by side on the sofa were three girls of about fifteen in white blouses, soft-skinned things, chattering and fidgeting. Before they saw me they jumped up laughing and came one after the other to look down the road; then, as quickly, they sat down. One had glasses, and a blue skirt, another, a saffron skirt, and the other, a grey. They looked at me variously, without much curiosity, happy. The one who watched me longest was still laughing at whatever had amused them earlier.

Today I do not wish to go out. I should see too much in this sunlight. This holiday is bent on turning into something, and I am disturbed lest it should be a panic and a retreat. The days are dangerous to me; deserted beaches, withdrawals of sensation. If I go out today or tomorrow while it is light, I shall be forced to seek out somebody I know. If I go out tonight, I think I can remain alone. I shall dream on my feet, then.

35.

Night. A tall sky, deep blue, with a few metallic stars glittering, well away from the moon. The moon high and still, no clouds anywhere. Past midnight. Most of the lamps out here; steely sky towering over everything.

The main streets almost void now. I meet nobody. No reason for anybody to come down here. A windless cold prickles my scalp and turns the ridges of the warehouses to black cast-iron. The furnaces are all out; three days, and the smoke's gone. Hours of moonlight have washed the noises away. A horizon two miles across the valley, where the railway goes; I can see the packed buildings, and suggestions of colour.

Downhill, towards the viaduct. The last gaunt concrete towers of the new offices jut over the slope behind me. Road builders' machines here, rolls of wire mesh. The streets are all changed.

It is still there. Between the hoardings, a narrow opening, completely dark. I have not looked for it since I left it that Sunday, a long while ago. But the first part will be familiar.

Cold, narrow, echoing. A lamp, but no light. The tall blue walls rearing straight. The creek of the sky. Should I mind its regard? The moon out of sight somewhere behind the station and a couple of stars squinting over.

Clean cobbles; no horses any more. I can assume complete disuse. At any rate, nobody lingers, nobody notices. The door to the graveyard. No. I go on. It would be just if nothing should happen, and I looked forward to immediate anti-climax.

That bird. A flutter in my mind. Neither that. The wide street I rode along, lost; lit now in hideous green. One lorry. Across the street, by the arch, the resumption, the trenched incline plunging more steeply from its narrow re-opening. From here on I know nothing. I do not know whether another street ever crosses.

Here the viaduct wall, growing ever higher, leans back, with buttresses. On my left, still a featureless wall, with iron spikes along its crest. Steep, a clangorous echo of my steps from the darkness ahead, like an oildrum. The street is gone now. Darkness before and behind. Only the sky stares.

Slow. There is somebody behind that next buttress. Lovers. No, images. So; it is to be people: Little Margaret Claydon stands there, precise and firm on light heels, smiling agreeably at me, her grey eyes bright.

Hello Margaret. She does not answer. Good. Apparitions not messages. She's not cold there in her party frock. Fair hair in a swag. I like Margaret. Healthy and hard. She's poor Andrew's mistress. That is good; her strong mouth, his sick, bitten pallor. She's no fool. And it is good that she affects my taste for railway arches.

Stop. There are more. No concealment then, no surprise. I can see them ahead, on both sides, glimmering in the darkness, that flows and curdles in the brick-lined gut below, like tar.

Here is Sheila. Again still, again smiling. Large pale eyes, heavy face, long neck. A grey suit and a jersey. I need not speak, for clearly she will not. I've not seen her since the abortion. She looks very well after it. I suppose Millward will have slunk off by now, rubbing his scrubby hair. But she will look after herself. She leans out a little way towards me as I pass, her face coming forward, grinning agreeably like a cat.

How contented they are: to be standing in a tight street like this. They do not let the enormous walls dwarf them.

And as I walked between them the prospect alters; they seem to be standing at the doorways and windows of ruined houses, silhouetted against the sky, framed in the broken facades. I did not know there were so many benign spirits in my life. I have met these girls with friends only at odd times during the past month or two, and I had not realised how similar they were. There is a taste of clean silk, and independence, about all of them. They sit in the cafés in the afternoons. They know everybody.

Joan Mason leaning out of a gutted window, her soft elbows on the stone sill. Pudgy sardonic features, little eyes; comfortable, comforting. The lone wolf. Yes, they have drifted together here in my mind. Moonlight, serene air, cold cobbles.

UNDER THE VIADUCT

Still dark, no sound of any kind. Behind me I feel softness. Before me there is nothing much. Walls again on either side. Nobody about. The sky somewhat greyer, high above, and the steep slope underfoot becoming more even as I go on. I have almost reached the bottom.

No. Not humiliation after all this. I have not come here to be made juvenile again. I just came past an unlit lamp post, and now two middle-aged harlots from the Crown are walking along beside me, one on either side. There is just room for them. Mrs Edna Howes and Mrs May Johnson. It is no use my trying to shake them off; I can see I have done that once too often.

I look sidelong at them. They do not attempt to catch my eye, but both walk with heads lifted a little, eyes averted under demure lids, lips pursed. They have a purposeful air of quiet triumph. They are leading me homeward towards morning. And what is morning to either of them? Do they think they are my mother's breasts?

We are on level ground and the walls are lower. It is not so dark, and I am filled with the physical sense of their presence; heavy with it; sluggish. Mrs May Johnson, on my right, wears a loose black coat and a little feathered hat. Her neat hair is dyed black and her heavy, cruel face is painted with art. Her big black rimmed glasses glitter, hiding her eyes. Thin lips curved in satisfaction and disgust. Heavy shoulders jostling me, without suggestion. She is nearly as tall, on her skinny black heels, as I am. Mrs Edna Hayes is short and broad, grey suited and blonde with a pretty face so exaggerated as to be coarse, grotesque; big blue eyes, awkwardly outlined and blinking, a curved nose, and a wide pouting red mouth tucked in at the corners. The face and the lined throat coated with a dark powder; little hairs on the upper lip. I look down on the soft roll of bosom in the white satin blouse.

Nothing is happening. We are simply walking forward. They are not doing anything to me; am I of them? Have I become like them, soft and frigid?

My clothes are unchanged. My body is still mine. But I cannot separate myself, walking thus, from the awareness of the round smooth-stockinged legs moving on either side of me, the dulled flesh, the stumping gait, the pasty skin of the thighs, the tight apparatus of clothing stretching and rustling. I feel it all in my own skin, like bruising. There was scent, of course, pale, opaque and meaningless; but also the odours of dusty corners of dressing tables and wardrobes from years ago. Furniture-polish, toilet soap, stout. Aches and pains.

Mrs Hayes breaks wind softly against her corsets. These old trollops want me; they have wanted me since they first saw me. These are the two who realised, of all the whores in the town, what it was that brought me, day after day, to watch them at work. These are the two who knew from an early moment, that I would neither go with them nor go away and forget their existence. They have not been friendly; they do not like my gaze upon them. But they understand it, they know they attract me because I can tell they despise the sexual act. Mrs Johnson despises it with a certain brutal narcissism; Mrs Hayes with a kind of slapdash abandon that is reflected in the clownish splendour of her façade.

They have not enjoyed being looked at in this way for so long; they have been put out. But I had thought they had grown accustomed to it, and bored. I did not think they had it in them to plan an advance that would appeal to me, a difficult customer; they haven't the ambition, usually, to cater for perversions of any kind.

So what do they offer to me? Neither of them can rouse me to desire what they would expect me to desire in her, nor make me available to her as what she would regard, curiously enough, as a man. Neither of them can provide anything for which I'd pay, even so much as half a crown. Not even their autobiographies; no surprises there, no illuminations.

They offer me membership. Assimilation. Osmotic exchange of identities, sensations, attitudes. It is happening now as we pace the level floor of the lampless gulley. It has been happening for a very long time. I am becoming a middle-aged prostitute. Well, well.

I once considered such a metamorphosis; it was a day-dream I would divert myself with during boring lessons at school. The change seemed full of possibilities. But now the diffuse-presence of my two companions robs it of all salacity. They are taking me where I shall be freed from sexuality: to a bay-windowed house in an Edwardian row, with coloured glass in the fanlight, and pink net curtains. There we shall cook for one another out of tins and read out bits of the newspaper. I shall have a coldly-lit bedroom over the little back garden; a dressing table with embroidered runners, I suppose, and green glass trays; a rather high bed with a shiny eiderdown and a little lamp over the headboard. I shall have to have a sizeable chamber pot, too, and at least three drawers full of cold underwear. What loneliness! Whatever they do to my mind, I shall still know that loneliness, which will be my own, not drawn from them. The loneliness of the pretty clothes that do not attract because they are mine already; the loneliness of the afternoon bus journeys, with gloves and handbag, that always lead to the same place.

Yet maybe they will bring my work to me, at first, anyway. I cannot imagine it, yet. Their silence has told me nothing about it. Do they know anything? Shall I be given any guidance in how to think of it or will it always be a kind of anaesthetic blank, smiling though faceless, through which the edges of my senses will sometimes be fated to wake?

This is where I fear I shall betray myself. I can live day in day out like an old whore, in between times. I can talk to the others in this cosy liberation from desire. But shut in that room with the shiny eiderdown, making myself somewhat flaccidly available to these suddenly confidential men – and I can see them easily enough, undersized, or expansive and elderly, or fiercely nervous, paralytically curious, all juvenile in their approach and all of a certain class with an upper limit clearly defined at about the level of a bus inspector – shut in that room with the ludicrous thing happening, causing me, maybe, more discomfort than usual, I can imagine being suddenly born back into myself again, and finding that I existed only in a few parts of a strange body fifty years old; a fattened wrist, a shaved, crinkly armpit dabbed with powder, gums that had dental plates and an unfamiliar flavour. No more. Only the sensation, everywhere but in these few points of sense, of an enormous boredom, dominant, physically personified, importunately intrusive.

We seem to have come a long way together. The place is quite featureless, but the sky seems lighter, and although there seems to be no external change in any of us – they are still trotting along, pleasantly possessive – it is maybe near the time when we shall emerge into the suburb where that Edwardian house is.

O where is that fate for which I dream? I am not here to lose myself, or to find myself as the prisoner of a wardrobe! These are merely my tired fears.

Nothing I really want would be so far down here, in this faintly stinking darkness. Yet I have come to it.

They are gone. Mrs Johnson and Mrs Hayes. Is it that the ways have divided? I cannot tell. It is growing lighter, grey and cold on the slate bricks, but I do not know what I see. I am not sure whether the walls still surround me. Those two have fallen from my eyes, from my two slack hands, with a twofold eructation they have left my lips. They will not return now.

This is the deadliest morning that is coming now. I can sense only the absence of the constraint of that long alley, the removal of the embankment, the widening of the floor, as far as makes no matter. If I could see things at all, I would be able to say I was in a flat, spreading, littered place, all made of low levels and inconsequential little vistas. I am glad to be thus blinded, robbed of all sensation for a while, for I do not wish to know anything of this morning. I have lost, without knowing what the victory might have been. Perhaps that knowledge was all I was after. I have lost, and the bitterness of that defeat, if I had senses to be possessed by it, would shrivel me and burst me.

As I stare, I see in my mind my staring eye. The cold curve, the greenish tints of the iris, characterise the air into which it gazes. And gradually, the vacancy breeds my location, drawing in outlines where I ask for them, telling me where is stone, where is iron.

I have come out into a great expanse of sidings. Nothing breaks the continuous flat levels of trucks except a gantry, a loading gauge or two, a water tower; far away, black sheds ride up above the colourless tide of wagons. I am in the middle of all this, standing in a cattle pen, one of an acre of cattle pens, iron barred, concrete floored with hollow channels running across; all clean and deserted. No smoke from the engine-shed, not a bird in the sky.

I strike the topmost of the rust-smeared rails before me, and hear the low, jumping sound of it careering erratically through the system of fences with a toneless, throbbing ring that lasts some while. It dies away to the left, and the momentary silence brings back to me a slur of traffic from behind the sheds. Through a gap I see for a moment the top of a bus move past, its windows still lit.

36.

Now that my brief holiday is over, and its events swallowed up in the blink of other people's eyes, I think I should not be too solemn about these images of mine, too pressed. Woman, bird, vest, ashes. I looked for the woman too soon, for instance, because I had time free for the task, and Spring was dangerously well advanced. I am sure I can understand that small cotton singlet before I shall ever understand her.

When I was about twelve years old I first came to know, through a new friend, a little boy called Brian Key. He was seven or eight, and had a sister a year or two younger. She was well built and bright-eyed, full of good spirits; she was fussy and excitable, with slanted eyes that would narrow to glittering chinks of laugher or indignation. They would burst in together upon a game of the older children, suddenly and at odd hours, perform a sort of rough and tumble act, and then, before they could be possessed, before their mood could be changed, they would be off. They were always in a hurry to go back home.

At first I was not so curious as to ask what it was that was strange about them and their home. They were the sort of children who, though vigorous and clean, always wore bizarre and poverty-stricken clothes. Brian, for instance, always had boots on, and a cheap ragged machine-knitted jersey, while the little girl, Margaret, usually had an ancient velvet party frock, roughly cut down to fit her, and thick brown stockings that were always slipping down. They looked at first glance like slum children but did not speak or act as if they were; and they lived in a perfectly ordinary terraced house with a bay window and a little front garden. They never mentioned their parents, though; and one had the feeling that for most of their lives they were imprisoned by some strange belief, some secret loyalty.

One day they were with us in the street, when the front door of their house opened and a tall woman with dark hair appeared. She wore an overall and had a worried pale face with protruding eyes. Catching sight of the children, she gestured to them, staring. Then she moved her lips wordlessly, exaggeratedly, while they watched. They made no sound. Finally she thrust out her hands and began making signs in a deaf-and-dumb alphabet. Immediately, as she closed the door, the children scuttled off up the entry way.

Then I asked questions of those who knew them. No, the woman was not their mother. They had no mother, she was their aunt. The mother was dead? Dead or gone away, the adults pretended not to know, said the others. The father lived somewhere else too.

Months later I saw the father. It was an early evening in late summer. The school holidays were nearly over, and we were all bored, sitting there on doorsteps, cracking jokes, taunting one another in the tired sunlight. The Key children had been with us, but had disappeared, an hour ago or more. Then I saw them peeping through the curtains of the bay window, not at us but at the end of the street. They retired, and came back to their places again, several times.

Then at last the door burst open and they burst out. A man of medium height, in sports coat and flannels, with a raincoat folded over his arm, had come round the corner and was approaching the house. He was tanned and sprightly, with thinning hair brushed back. The children, in their ragged clothes dashed up the street towards him, shouting; the deaf-and-dumb woman ran out after them worried and smiling, then retired to the doorway.

The little boy and girl hurled themselves upon their father who stopped, winded and amazed. Faces appeared behind lace curtains all along the street, and the other children stopped playing to watch. Mr Key seized his daughter and threw her into the air, caught her and tucked her, kicking, under his arm. The boy jumped up, arms round his neck, knees struggling to climb. Somehow the man took both children, one in each arm and lifted them from the ground; they clung to him fast, hugging his shoulders, burying their faces in his jacket, rubbing their heads against him. Unsteadily he walked towards the house, carrying the two; as he went, he muzzled their heads with his chin, and his raincoat trailed on the pavement.

I remember the sight made me cry, where I skulked behind the privet bushes in somebody's front garden. The rest? It makes me think more of the Brian Key I knew in later years – but let it stand for the pathos of that moment.

* * *

[...] have all been razed flat, rises almost directly above the street where my father was born, the street down which the boy ran with his bathing suit and towel, the street whose sights and sounds of a lifetime ago rest now once more in the ancient head, with its vacant face. Let them confront each other there in the sunshine in that open space above their home; let it be their home now, for the street, though probably little altered, will be loud with strangers. They can remain there for a while. They can remain together for ever, as they must; I know the city well enough to find new places for their silent discourse when I need.

Establishing them there, and pleased with my work, I am eager to bring the girl to join them, but I see at once that it will not do. Her face floats in the morning air, evasively, giving them the same indulgent, furtive regard she gave me. That is too private, too quick; it is too much my own affair to be mingled with the dialogue of the others. And, seeing this, I realise how completely I am excluded from the scene I have made. Whatever the old man has to tell the boy, I do not figure in the story except as a marginal character, of no interest. That gives me relief; my part is over.

53.

Brick-dust in sunlight. That is what I see now in the city, a dry, vibrant epic flavour, whose air is human breath. A place of walls made straight with plumbline and trowel, to desiccate and crumble in the sun and the smoke. Blistered paint on cisterns and girders, cracking to show the priming. Old men spit on the paving-slabs, little boys urinate, and the sun dries it, as it dries out the patches of damp on plaster facings, leaving misshapen dyed stains.

I frequent this quarter, now decayed, where he was born, a place where there is hardly any vegetation but tufts of grass in disused alleyways, an occasional bush of mimosa in a forecourt. I have found the street, and the house. Among his papers was the birth certificate and the bond of his apprenticeship; both bore an address in a street I had never heard him mention. I had not known of its presence. It is a long steep street, quite wide, lined with terraces of severe three-storied houses, their doors opening straight onto the pavements. Only behind a few of them are there gardens; for the most part the entryways open into courts of back-to-back dwellings, with rows of wash houses and privies. The street plunges down to join what was once the main road into the city; on fine mornings the sun shines across into it, dazzling gold on the blackened houses. This is one of those areas where nobody has thought it worthwhile to change anything, in nearly a hundred years, where the houses are so solidly built, however, that they stand firm in their grime and show few signs of the passage of time. Looking at the house where he was born, I can, without altering a single detail, go back to the period of his boyhood and beyond. The panelled door, with its worn paint and heavy knocker, is the original; the curtains at the broad windows are plain and nondescript. It costs me no trouble to see the four children of the picture passing in and out; I cannot avoid doing so. I can see this house as it was before it began to live. The morning sunlight, the ponderous brickwork; on a Sunday, when the streets are quiet.

In this city, that is made up so much of movement, where even opinions are made ductile and yielding by the tug and strain of what passes as events, I look for age. It is not for nothing that the figure of that aged man had itself transposed into the suburban garden in my vision of last December. By age, I do not mean the hoariness of the few ancient buildings that still stand hereabouts, or the historian's records of the days when this was a small country town. Those have, in fact, the disarming freshness of colour prints in a children's history book; they are not to my purpose.

I look for things that make old men and dead men seem young. I find them in the oldest parts of factories, in canal bridges, the walls of the infirmary, the giant buttresses of the slaughterhouse: things which have escaped, the landscapes of uncountable childhoods. Tarred gable ends, tenements more stout than any of the lives they have held, rearing their windows to take the sun over lower roofs. Soot, sunlight, brick-dust, idle, unceasing wind of breath.

54.

Even before he woke, he knew he was better, or had the promise of recovery. He came to his senses slowly, and opened his eyes late. When he finally knew he was conscious he found himself repeating. 'There must be a god in it' – a partial and individual god for every person, every thing, every act; a perfection, or at least a satisfaction to the senses, in each grouping of his understanding. While his eyes were still shut he was aware of colours, flakes, gobbets and banners of colour, which moved, symbolic of satisfaction and understanding, in a void of half-perceived shapes. And, at times, when he willingly took the message of the colours and felt his mind moving towards life as if in cold clear air, even the void held something that shone, as mahogany or copper shines in semi-darkness.

55.

I can hardly believe that these moments of peace, of sensual hope, are truly mine, and so I cannot talk of them possessively, in the first person.

One reason I find it hard to admit them as mine is that they seem to ask more of me than I think I have to give. One glimpse of an imagined world changes my whole life. Everything in my life that makes some sort of order possible might have to follow the commands of the mere hint of an unknown colour or an enigmatic scent, and in the pursuit might be gathered up as a garment puckers round a drawstring; it might be wrinkled into an impossible tangle if the clue should be false.

And why should the clues be otherwise? I do not suppose them to be more than fragments of dream that are attracted by the passivity I sometimes indulge in while waking.

I think that pursuit is not the way. I am not, after all, searching for an end; for a state, rather, a condition in which I can believe myself alive. The finality I look for is not in myself, for I do not love death, but in my perception. Often now, in solitude, I see things that appear to me as final, that [...]

*   *   *

61.

Tonight walking late past a group of office buildings I saw, on a massively pillared porch a large nameplate. The broad gilt letters said: 'THE IMPERIAL GROUP'. Nothing else. Nothing, such as 'Branch Headquarters' or 'X & Y Limited, Area Representative' that might have detracted from the monolithic menace of the title. There was a time in early childhood when I would have regarded such titles as valid projections of a paternal image, as real though mysterious forces. I know people who would still think of them in this way. Yet now I am cynical. I can see them only as facades for childishness and bungling duplicity. Yet they mean something, they still stir me a little as they did when I was a child. What it is, I think, is that I regard the mere fact of their existence as authoritative. It is a world of projections, without projectors. The projectors are people like myself, with similar makeup and motives. There is nothing grand about them. But there is a grandeur about what they make in their efforts at concealment.

62.

England. So well-mapped, so thoroughly documented. How can we exaggerate anything with the sea all around? Without a hinterland full of mysteries?

The English lack the temperamental helplessness of other European peoples: the Germans have to be Germanic, the French Gallic and so on. The English can believe they are anything. They have too few predispositions.

We are a nation of devourers. When things reach us, we pretend they have at last come home.

The country is too small. However freely the national good sense radiates from the capital, it can still reach the furthest outposts and neutralise them. There is no room for an answer to be evolved.

The metropolis is too large, the aristocracy of it too liberally distributed among small fry.

I want to remain in this city, looking for times and places that are unaccounted for, hoping that I too may escape the watchful eye of the nation.

63.

In the art gallery here there is a small broken Indian statue, of about the thirteenth century. The figure of a girl dancer, or rather, the torso, for the head and neck are missing, both arms are cracked-off just below the shoulders, and the legs are both lost, the left finishing just above the knee, the other a little higher. The right breast has been smashed; the nipple of the other worn away.

Even without the extremities that once will have given it artistic meaning, the body, with its long, supple waist and round thighs, holds grace. The shoulders are held a little way back, and the belly is thrust forward, swung to one side. Looking at this relic, one is not tempted to guess at the positions of the vanished head and limbs.

It is clothed only in festoons of ornate decorations, metal and stones against the soft flesh which now, its stone polished transformed by age into myriad roughenings and craters, looks porous and sleepy. There is a broad collar with heavy pendants, one of which, a triple rope of what seem to be pearls, falls sidelong to the waist. A necklace of similar design is cast loosely about the shoulders and falls through the deep hollow of the bosom. Just above the break in the left upper arm there is a tight circlet that rises in the shape of a crown. The hips are circled by a low deep belt that reaches to the loins: it starts with a tight flat band, of gold maybe, chased with circling patterns and then loosens into thick swathes and bands, of intricate design, falling low at the front and gathered up neatly at the hips. From this belt hang a central tasselled loop, heavy with baubles, that passes freely between the legs, and also the decorations of the thighs, pendants of beaten metal stretching down toward the vanished knees. Dangling between these and the belt are heavy braided loops hung with medallions, several bands of them, the higher ones loosely curved, the lower clasping the limbs more closely.

Robbed of its gestures and its face, and thus of the appearance of mind, the body is dominated, not by this single breast, but by the large and beautiful navel, thrust out and held up into a pout by the constricting belt that curves close beneath it. It is very slightly oval, stretched not upwards but out across the belly. If the figure were life-sized the palm of a hand could only just cover its hollow, that begins very gradually, then plunges evenly into a deep shadow, ridged at the edge by a last flat fold of skin. This is the only feature the body possesses. It is eye, mouth or ear; it expresses in its simple enigmatic cavity, the nature of all the bodies orifices. Yet in itself it is useless, a scar crater, a mere insignia of the entrance to life. The gross and handsome decoration of the body rides among the luxuriant ornaments of the goldsmiths.

V

64.

Walking through the suburbs at night [...] as I pass the dentist's house, I hear a clock chime a quarter, a desolate brassy sound. I know where it stands, on the mantelpiece in the still surgery. The chime falls back into the house, and beyond it, without end. Peace.

I sense the simple nakedness of these tiers of sleeping men and women beneath whose windows I pass. I imagine it in its own setting, a mean bathroom in a house no longer new, a bathroom with plank panelling, painted a peculiar shade of green by an amateur, and badly preserved. It is full of steam, so much as to obscure the yellow light and hide the high, patched ceiling. In this dream, standing quiet, the private image of a householder or his wife, damp and clean.

I see this as it might be floating in the dark, as if the twinkling point of a distant streetlamp had blown in closer, swelling and softening to a foggy oval. I can call up a series of such glimpses, that need have no end, for they are all the bodies of strangers. Some are deformed or diseased, some are ashamed, but the peace of humility and weakness is there in them all. They have the factual undramatic flavour of the Stations of the Cross posted unobtrusively round the walls of a Catholic church. The story they tell is an old one.

I have often felt myself to be vicious, in living so much by the eye, and among so many people. I can be afraid that the egg of light through which I see these bodies might present itself as a keyhole. Though I can find no sadism in the way I see them now. They have the warm flesh of a Renoir, yet their shapes have the minuscule, remote morality of some mediaeval woodcut of the Expulsion; an eternally startled Adam, a permanently bemused Eve. I see them as homunculi, moving privately each in a softly lit fruit hung in a nocturnal tree. I can consider without envy or scorn the well-found bedrooms I pass, walnut and rose-pink, altars of tidy, dark haired women, bare backed, wifely. Even in these I can see order.

65.

*   *   *

[…] these companions, and let their own personalities go free.

66.

One of the reasons for my admiration of the Giantess is the delicate strategy with which she controls the born body, that is so huge and so demanding.

I am trying to find my way. How do the others answer to this kind of questioning? The whores come as near to conquering that body as possible. They govern it by capricious force. The young women I meet, the eyes of the cafés – they are still hoping their bodies will mean what they want them to mean. By the cool eagerness of their minds they hold them back. The stone woman and the girl I have been seeking have controlled the mute body by a straining of the will, and in them a duality begins to appear. That duality is most marked in the three strange women I first thought of as tragic but now consider to be in states of constant […]

* * *

[…] thing like […] shown the day before I should need to be confident and pleasant. I tried to relax, but I could not. I felt as callow and apprehensive as I had felt at fourteen.

I sat where I could see people coming up the stairs, and where I could be seen, growing more confused at each new entry.

* * *

[…] somewhere, long ago. Lasted only a second; the attempt did not engage her, and I am convinced that as we passed she saw me as a complete stranger.

69.

The Bull of Night. I give to the night of the city a foreign image, that of a black long-horned bull, whose giant body in the sky contains us, in one of the whorls of light that mark the tips of his horns, or his eyes or his hooves. In him the city is small, tender and bright, a helpless thing, joined to him only by the sullen weight of unknown energy it holds. With him, it does not swing through its own smoky sky or through any English air, but through some remote and foreign element. At night, the customs of the place fade and fall apart, leaving only the suggestions of the lights. The slow movements of the bull encourage me to follow up these suggestions. I can suppose that his obscure and incorporeal shape moves either among the stars, or can be seen extending beyond the scattered lights of the city that forms part of him. I can imagine his red eyes goggling low in the sky or out along the railway tracks. He is the most frivolous and ancient of the gods with whom I replace the god of England. I can imagine him only when the day has receded far from the stony arena of midnight, all time-things fallen away, the drip of a cistern building up a pattern only to drop back again and again to its beginning. In him, some things are possible. He is like intoxication; once he comes into being one can expect to move within him forever, in his suppleness and warmth, without ever coming out for judgement.

..... An orderly underground bar full of men, towards closing time. If I close my eyes, I move from a small, brightly-lit room of brown wood and red leather into the crazy caverns of his body. Into a world of spaciousness, and of deep sound that comes in several suggested dimensions. No sight, except a sense of epic underground light on my eyelids. Then odours come, and I am fetched off into memory, memories not of actual things but of imagined ones, or at moments I feel that what I am imagining is masquerading as memory. In this sightlessness I feel great wakefulness and pleasure of the senses.

I see beasts thundering along in the fog among railway wagons with coloured lamps in their heads. A furnace door opens and a blast of voices comes out with the glare. There are gantries and jibs that climb up among one another's girders, threaded with globular lights that glow, bobbing, in the murk of dusk.

I feel my fingers numb with thoughts. My mind tunes itself approximately to a certain pitch level and hears certain sliding sequences of tones, rising and falling seconds, eddying gradually up and down like drunken songs, as the various speaking voices in the room strike the tones in passing. The sequences of voices have a pattern, a long shallow curve, shaped like the arc of a gong. Over the top of this hollow copper music, a sudden whistle hops up and down like a paper bird.

I have no sense of the walls. The limit of the world is smoke, rolling in the distance, trailing between the horns of the bull......

The bull is capricious and foreign. Often I hope I shall wake into my own city and find that it has, without changing, become a foreign place, whose delights are new. Yet I would not have the fears and [...]

From a *Citizen* notebook

(1960)

10.xi.60

There's something to be salvaged from all this. But it must have a clear and dominant tone, and that tone must be the physical presence of the city.

It is the symbol of a variable, but limited, state of mind.

In the book as I planned it, there is too much *furor poeticus*, too much gas and flesh. The point should be that while I am involved in the city, which is in a sense myself, I cannot approach woman. The streets contain the soft white drawers, the soft belly, the pretty voice with its accent; but much later[.]

Vera Reynolds is the woman the city as I see it in a certain mood produces. Especially again, the white underwear, the massive legs – and the wrecked mind.

Only when the city is turned to art can the casual woman become possible.

The attempt to approach Vera is a black and white bottleneck, from which this realisation emerges. The memory of her is aesthetic. A concentration of non–erotic physical [illegible].

The book must be scrubbed of all humour or indulgence, so that love can enter it, a sort of appetite that is suited to dedication.

Avoid the supernatural and the journalistic alike. Externalise as much as possible. Erase all possibility of an explanation of everything in the light of the narrator's Freudian condition.

He is as he is because he is involved with the city. He does not love the city merely because he cannot seduce women.

Don't pander to curiosity about this. No need to say he has had women, or hasn't. The quality of his life is as it is, is what matters. If this is presented as a solid, the thing ceases to be a *bildungsroman* and becomes an examination. Being is taken for granted, Becoming is treated as weakness.

The Recurrence and Accumulation phenomena, for instance – the piled pennies – these override the introspective sequence, the moralising commentary.

The only change in the book is the gradual increase in externalisation[.]

The book is about the way in which one apprehends reality.

11.xi.60

No escape from the city.

No hint of perpetual sunshine. The city will not dissolve.

The citizen shall not invite pity. All that he asks for is to be trusted. His trustworthiness must be apparent.

He must find local equivalents for his romantic moments, and stand aside from them. That is why he falls in love.

The book must drive towards an ending that is like the radiator of an old car, the face of a diesel engine, the window-dentures of a grey modern factory. It must become increasingly solid as it drives.

None of this springtime mood. End in winter. Or obliterate all time tracks in the last third of the book.

The power of the old is found in the new. That is the particular power of traction of images the book sets out to exert.

A flat roof, not a barrel vault. A long quartet, not a gothic symphony on a small scale. Upper and lower limits closer together than I had at first imagined.

After the Vera Reynolds episode, and its splintering, there is to be no significant action. The long last movement is to be a run of Supposes, into which the narrator is released by his earlier examination of facts.

For I want to describe and reproduce consciousness – not symbolise it and dramatise it: (we be not Novelists here, Mister. Let you be open with me.)

Thus the movement is from one of extravagant assertion to one of moderate but continuously available supposition. The interpreter of reality puts forward the hypotheses of creation.

Little fragments of narrative, as in the Cantos. Short-breathed sections that are no longer essays. Bits of conversation. A breaking out of the central consciousness into a multiplicity. The statue over the *Woodman*'s door. An egg.

Move from *Dubliners* via the usual channels to *Finnegans Wake*, I suppose. But I want to spike my material out through the skin of the baggy & steamy human consciousness. The frightful comic claustrophobia of *Finnegans Wake* (however all-embracing it is) is what I'm out to cut across. I aspire more.

It seems to me that nobody likes what Joyce did, although they can see the relevance of his methods. Nobody has covered the same (essential) ground and reached a different conclusion.

Five uncollected *City* poems

(*c.* late 1950s)

The Fog at Birmingham

Shrouded invisible in fog
      at midday standing
Silently ten yards
      above the wagon-factory's roof,
I am the sun's firstborn you find so terrible.

I have found out my place
Over this backyard valley where I was born
    And where so many thousands
Live, and a thousand thousand in the meadows beyond,
Seamed down with brick all over and iron and edgeless smiles.

    Over in the massive cemetery
The legions of the dead are spent and bleak
    As the eyes of pigeons
      awake before the human dawn;

I know how corpses are laid
      carefully by
So that they can stare and spin
      all into their proper places
When the turf sheet ripples and bursts
      on Resurrection morning,
    But this place I have found
By rising blindly into it on life's coldest days
    Is found in no way
      for the mesh and hooks of death:

It is my place for the hours of First Creation.

It is found in fog, and milky weather:
                    I have seen,
Have stood looking over this city
                    from the little waste plain
Above where the curving railway
Bites its long sour furrow up into the west:

   I have seen the city as a bowl
                    filled with peace,
Its nearby turbulence of lines,
                    pangs of dark terraces,
softened among the fading reaches;

                    I have seen it
   The solid roofs' tideway,
Fingering points of light through wintry haze;

And I have seen the spots of blood on the soft feathers of its wings.

So many things would vanish, lapped up into a moving element,
While light came like a lance
                    or a hollow voice relentlessly talking;
and what it struck, or spoke of – what shapes it sought out of the
                                        vapour –
Seemed to enclose for me
                    tenderly among their sombre lines
                         the glades of peace:
   Times flaked off from my life
                    and from the pain I knew
When the sun's thick palm
   Was thrust down hard all day
                    on the fired streets

Pressing the city down
       among its own underground furnaces –
'Because,' says the air,
'Being so feminine, it needed the force.' –

When, outlined among my outlined million,
       I could be
No more than another annealed cavity, a shard,
       cut down into the ground.

I am the sun's child only
       in dull red, grey-streaked times;
   This place I found for First Creation
Requires not retrospect but murky weather.

I am not concerned with Time,
   How it handles us;
Creation is now, and is not yet.

       And for me
This now, when the painful city
Clamped in the unmoving hands of wind and sun
Fumbles itself in dirt and cloud
       so that I can walk
From between bleared walls clean into great Nothing,
Thunderous with rolling swathes of life
       and gongs of light far in the distance,
Is a day when I am made, and the unguessed world.

And I am made the sun's firstborn
       in the top of the fog
   Where he begins to show

Faintly through the slowly spinning mists
                              his pallid body,
Cold like a fish, and comfortless and true.

Midlanders

We are the tenants here of something which, unseen,
in its turn inhabits us and our breath and makes
the countryside we've never lived in seem like home;
and sometimes, for a moment, it humiliates the strong father before
                                                    his children:
they don't see it, but they begin to learn its ways.

Walking here you become obsessed
by the chaste droppings of this abstract:
                              nothing that putrefies
                    nothing that does
more than glisten in the rain, scuffle its dust,
            dry the sweat on your windows;

if it stank, somebody would do something about it.

It drops in two kinds
            according to its diet:
spoilbanks and cemeteries.

                    And what
could be chaster than the tip?
            whose arid stirrings
are the civilised gossip of dead fields.

There are dead men too.
            Many sieved into cigar boxes,
some shrivelled unimaginably under marble carpentry;

and often on derelict sites weeds snake
               across the grit floors,
                    the sodden backs of tombs,
mossy, are choked with tall grasses,
                the rain, among old kilns,
makes chains of ponds;

and when lupins grow wild and the cats play
among the graves' alleys – then you can remember the dead,
know how they are occupied underfoot: you ask –
'These stagnant pools, this mouldering; are they the stench
that betrays the devourer?'

              'There's been nobody here of that description; everyone
                      thinks of this
as the country these days. The wild flowers,
              sunshine, sparrows in the holly bushes
show that these people died happy; or at least
they're all right now.'

Sea Monster in Hospital Shed

The journalists heard of it too late,
When even the odour was gone
And the shed dismantled.

Stories? There were stories;
Lightly related – all agreed
It was an interesting episode.

Outpatients remembered slithering sounds
In the green shed by the ambulance park –
Had thought it something official.

Some of the doctors had seen it alive:
A thing the size of a cow, they said;
Lethargic, stentorious, its eyes out of focus.

A caretaker had hosed it down twice daily
And the bursar had had it well fed with scraps,
Until they were both advised to discontinue this treatment.

It had languished on through December
And into the New Year; the staff
No longer cared to be seen peering in.

In fact, when it died, quietly in its corner,
It lay several days unattended.
Nobody would admit to having looked at it.

As the end approached, it had become much smaller;
But those who were called to remove it
Found it quite damp, and extremely heavy.

Its death was ascribed to malnutrition
And desiccation to a lesser extent:
Autopsy was dispensed with.

As there was no record of its first admission,
Or of its having bequeathed itself for purpose of study,
its remains were disposed of by incineration.

The furnaceman had no clear memory of it,
And was flippant, to say the least, with enquirers –
The matron and superintendent were far more reasonable.

Where We Are

From a little distance, from the first suburb
Across the first slight valley,
The city's giant rows commingle
Minute and tottering,
Obscure streets' petty governors,
Far from the sky.

No more than this. The concrete keys
Jangle a hand tattoo
Tapped baldly out of music heard
At several removes
In home-made avenues that required
No conqueror's plan.

This is a fleck of a civilisation,
A spat froth that's congealed
And lies across the earth, and breeds
Us, who can be no more
Than creatures of an authority
Nowhere to be found.

And amateurs, frock-coated peasants,
Dictate the laws and build;
These, and the wandering officials
From the now-vacant centre,
Some generations out from home,
Playing at order.

This place, for all its bird–splashed statues,
Never saw greatness, nor
Was memory's root uncovered here;
This is not where they happened,
The culture's solemn anecdotes,
Nor will it be.

Nor will it be. And so there's room
Under the thick-brained sky
For life to shake itself, unseen,
And run the streets by day,
Insane with pure locality;
Shouting for poets.

Lost, Now

Let us live dangerously, like the houses
That give up trying to discover what district they live in;
Whose surroundings can never summon the power to claim them.

Like them, we feel beneath us
Only the rubble-filled hollows
Of land long enervated,

And lie in one of those suburbs of the soul
That have no roof-brain and are dumb;

Where on the yellow summer mornings
The long curves of the streets sag out of shape,
And where at night the lamps
Convert the air to a grey marsh of disquiet.

So let us turn the pages of the weather,
Not troubling ourselves to see
Whether the book be upside-down or no.

And trap the world's explosive breath
When, grown diffuse and far too careless,
It drifts at last defenceless down the gutters;

We'll make it talk for us and through us,
And disregard the wounds its words make
On these soft lips with which we try to kiss.

CITY

(1961)

Preface

What follows seems to me a ruined work of art. It lies around as a series of sketches might lie around a studio waiting in vain for the total act of sculpture they were drawn to serve. Yet I am glad the writer has made no attempt to give it a bogus unity, but has preferred to leave it as it stands. What it has to say it will say to those who can see where it was aiming: if it had been tidied up the gesture it does make towards a total structure would have got obscured.

Unity is hard to come by, anyway, at the depth at which this writing is operating. There are cases where love of humanity best shows itself in a desperate exposure of personal nakedness – Lear's Fool and Edgar in the storm – than in a willed uplift. The world of the last forty years is one in which whatever unity that was achieved in Central Europe was at the expense of the suffering and ultimate death of six million people in concentration camps, and in which the unity of the communist world would have been impossible without the continuous presence of twenty million people in forced labour camps, and the premature death, by starvation or worse, of at least as many as were exterminated by the Germans. These things must not be forgotten in talking politics or sociology. Even in my placid area south-west of Birmingham the intake into the mental hospital is such that in a twenty-year period a fifth of the population will have had some treatment either as inpatients or outpatients. Modern industrial society seems to need its scapegoats. At their best the writers of the West have had this kind of knowledge in their bones, and their struggles after unity can no more be written off as due to their faulty politics than can the suicides of Mayakowsky, Esenin, or Tsvetayeva.

In approaching *City*, I find myself forced again to ask questions about other works of art, where I have found similar difficulties. In what ways do *The Waste Land*, *Ulysses*, and the *Cantos* of Ezra Pound fail to have that inner order which is the essential of a completed work of art? Does it matter if they don't?

The fact is that for thirty-five years these works have been seen as magnificent dead-ends – so much so that many writers have tried to go on as though they had never existed. In a curious way a generous admiration of these works has served cowardice, has inhibited further attempts on the same area which they were working. Yet the position of these works seems to me to be more analogous to the place that Zeta holds in thermo-nuclear research. They can be made use of only in the negative way of sensing how their failure finally bars certain approaches, and by implication shows up more clearly the necessity of others. Fisher's work seems to me a different attempt on the same area, but this time by a man who has been drawing on Pasternak and Mayakowsky.

The Waste Land is particularly difficult to absorb, because in it are traces of a genuine ordering, and it is easy to mistake the genuine for the bogus. According to Hugh Kenner what happened was that the poet found himself with a great deal of material in which he could not find inner coherence. Pound then made it cohere. What seems to have happened is that at the time Eliot was stumbling towards a way of allowing poetic material to order itself which he only gained control of later, when he wrote the poem 'Marina'. What genuine order there is in *The Waste Land* resembles that in 'Marina'. But the bluff at a genuine structure based on the Grail myth seems to be all Pound's. I do not blame Pound for the attempt – only the bluff. If Eliot could have finished the work then himself he would have done. I find Pound's *Cantos* more tragic, because in this case the bluffer has frustrated his own genius and not another's. Scattered around the *Cantos* are fragments of the work of a great poet: yet the organisation of the poems as a whole is all done with the conscious mind and the will; it is not organic. Pound seems to have taken his weakness for his strength, and almost wilfully denied his strength growth. I am not making judgements here: everyone has to work in the dark; it is only afterwards that it becomes clear just what was being done, and anyway at this level a magnificent failure gets farther than a superficial success.

Ulysses is a more complicated case than either of these. The formal organisation is there at so many levels: there is the image of Joyce poring over an enormous street-map of Dublin with an imaginary chronometer, getting the criss-crossings of his people in their Day right, and another of him looking around for some myth, some structure of events, to hang his whole undertaking on, and finding a series of parallel events to the search of Telemachus. And again the use of a different language to suit each section. Yet the work does fail to hold together: it doesn't achieve a total 'taking' of the city Dublin. There is no total effect that transcends and holds together the parts. All the work achieves is the disintegrated vision of a young failed Jesuit in the Stephen parts, together with fragments of a totally different vision, in the Leopold Bloom parts, of an attempt by the same man to understand what the non-seminary world is like. The work as a whole fails for the personal reason that Joyce himself failed to get into living contact with the 'ordinary' world, with the 'man-in-the-street'. It is no use the intellectual trying to do the ordinary world from the outside in this way. All he then achieves is a *conventional* view of what people are like. That it happens to be the convention that most people adopt most of the time doesn't mean for a moment that it represents what they are really like. People are far more than they represent to themselves. Ordinary people are not ordinary. Nor is the world. It is the business of an intellectual to see this. Not that he is any better than anyone else: only that he sees more. That is his gift. But to do this he must see for himself – not accept what ordinary people say they see. Joyce didn't use this gift: instead he chose 'silence, exile, and cunning'.

I do not say that *City* succeeds in any of the places I have thought these works to fail. Yet I find its existence changes the situation in a way which no critical work could do. The measure of its success is that by what it does manage to achieve it says, Look: Pound, Eliot, and Joyce didn't exhaust this area at all – it has been waiting all this time for someone with the courage to make a fresh bite. It proves this by actually taking the bite, not by talking about the desirability of doing so. If ever a work merited the description 'experimental writing' – in a good sense – this does.

MICHAEL SHAYER

Introduction

On one of the steep slopes that rise towards the centre of the city all the buildings have been destroyed within the past year: a whole district of the tall narrow houses that spilled around what were a hundred years ago outlying factories has gone. The streets remain, among the rough quadrilaterals of brick rubble, veering awkwardly towards one another through nothing; at night their rounded surfaces still shine under the irregularly-set gaslamps, and tonight they dully reflect also the yellowish flare, diffused and baleful, that hangs flat in the clouds a few hundred feet above the city's invisible heart. Occasional cars move cautiously across this waste, as if suspicious of the emptiness; there is little to separate the roadways from what lies between them. Their tail-lights vanish slowly into the blocks of surrounding buildings, maybe a quarter of a mile from the middle of the desolation.

And what is it that lies between these purposeless streets? There is not a whole brick, a foundation to stumble across, a drainpipe, a smashed fowl-house; the entire place has been razed flat, dug over, and smoothed down again. The bald curve of the hillside shows quite clearly here, near its crown, where the brilliant road, stacked close on either side with warehouses and shops, runs out towards the west. Down below, the district that fills the hollow is impenetrably black. The streets there are so close and so twisted among their massive tenements that it is impossible to trace the line of a single one of them by its lights. The lamps that can be seen shine oddly, and at mysterious distances, as if they were in a marsh. Only the great flat-roofed factory shows clear by its bulk, stretching across

three or four whole blocks just below the edge of the
waste, with solid rows of lit windows.

Lullaby and exhortation for the unwilling hero –

A fish,
Firelight,
A watery ceiling:
Under the door
The drunk wind sleeps.

– The bell in the river,
The loaf half eaten,
The coat of the sky –

A pear,
Perfume,
A white glade of curtains:
Out in the moonlight
The smoke reaches high.

– The statue in the cellar,
The skirt on the chairback,
The throat of the street –

A shell,
Shadow,
A floor spread with silence:
Faint on the skylight
The fat moths beat.

– The pearl in the stocking,
The coals left to die,
The bell in the river,
The loaf half eaten,
The coat of the sky.

The night slides like a thaw
And oil-drums bang together.

A frosted-glass door opening, then another.
Orange and blue décor.
The smoke that hugs the ceiling tastes of pepper.

What steps descend, what rails conduct?
Sodium bulbs equivocate,
And cowls of ventilators
With limewashed breath hint at the places
To which the void lift cages plunge or soar.

Prints on the landing walls
Are all gone blind with steam;

A voice under the floor
Swings a dull axe against a door.

The gaping office block of night
Shudders into the deep sky overhead:

Thrust down your foot in sleep
Among its depths. Do not respect
The janitors in bed,
The balustrades of iron bars,

The gusty stairwells; thrust it deep,
Into a concrete garage out of sight,
And rest among the cars
That, shut in filtered moonlight,
Sweat mercury and lead.

Subway trains, or winds of indigo,
Bang oil-drums in the yard for war:
Already, half-built towers
Over the bombed city
Show mouths that soon will speak no more,
Stoppered with the perfections of tomorrow.

You can lie women in your bed
With glass and mortar in their hair.
Pocket the key, and draw the curtains,
They'll not care.

Letters on a sweetshop window:
At last the rain slides them askew,
The foetus in the dustbin moves one claw.

And from the locomotive
That's halted on the viaduct
A last white rag of steam
Blows ghostly across the gardens.
When you wake, what will you do?

Under the floorboards of your dream
Gun barrels rolled in lint
Jockey the rooms this way and that.
Across the suburbs, squares of colour gleam:

Swaddled in pink and apricot,
The people are 'making love'.

Those are bright points that flicker
Softly, and vanish one by one.
Your telegraphic fingers mutter the world.
What will they reach for when your sleep is done?

The hiss of tyres along the gutter,
Odours of polish in the air;
A car sleeps in the neighbouring room,
A wardrobe by its radiator.

The rumbling canisters beat for you
Who are a room now altogether bare,
An open mouth pressed outwards against life,
Tasting the sleepers' breath,
The palms of hands, discarded shoes,
Lilac wood, the blade of a breadknife.

Before dawn in the sidings,
Over whose even tracks
Fat cooling towers caress the sky,
The rows of trucks
Extend: black, white,
White, grey, white, black,
Black, white, black, grey,

Marshalled like building blocks:

Women are never far away.

The Place – The Day

Where I was born, on the edge of the city a narrow road runs north from the main westward road into the small triangle of farmland that still separates the city from two of its neighbouring townships. After a couple of hundred yards it is joined by what was once a lane, but is now the last of the suburban streets. It has houses on one side and a cemetery on the other. Between the main road and this lane a large laundry was built in about 1930, a low brick building lying back from the roadway behind spiked railings and perfunctory gardens of lawn and laurel. The corner opposite the cemetery gate is now the laundry's car park; but before the war there was still the small yard of a monumental stonemason called McLean. It had a lean-to office with wide windows, a three-legged hoist with a dangling hook, and a neatly-gravelled patch, fenced off with loops of tarred chain between short marble posts, in which the completed tombstones were displayed for sale.

*

In the century that has passed since this city has become great, it has twice laid itself out in the shape of a wheel. The ghost of the older one still lies among the spokes of the new, those dozen loud highways that thread constricted ways through the inner suburbs, then thrust out, twice as wide, across the housing estates and into the countryside, dragging moraines of buildings with them. Sixty or seventy years ago there were other main roads, quite as important as these were then, but lying between their paths. By day they are simply alternatives, short cuts, lined solidly with parked cars and crammed with delivery vans. They look merely like side-streets, heartlessly overblown in some excess of Victorian expansion. By night, or on a Sunday, you can see them for what they are. They are still lit by gas, and the long rows of houses, three and four storeys high, rear black above the lamps enclosing the roadways, clamping them off from whatever surrounds them. From these pavements you can sometimes see the sky at night, not obscured as it is in most parts of the city by the greenish-blue haze of light that steams out of the mercury vapour lamps. These streets are not worth lighting. The houses have not been turned into shops – they are not villas either that might have become offices, but simply tall dwellings, opening straight off the street, with cavernous entries leading into back courts.

The people who live in them are mostly very old. Some have lived through three wars, some through only one; wars of newspapers, of mysterious sciences, of coercion, of disappearance. Wars that have come down the streets from the unknown city and the unknown world, like rainwater floods in the gutters. There are small shops at street corners, with whole faceless rows of houses between them; and public houses carved only shallowly into the massive walls. When these people go into the town, the buses they travel in stop just before they reach it, in the sombre back streets behind the Town Hall and the great insurance offices, or in the few streets that manage, on the sourthern side, to cross the imperious lines of the railway that fan out on broad viaducts from their tunnels beneath the central hill.

These lost streets are decaying only very slowly. The

impacted lives of their inhabitants, the meaninglessness of news, the dead black of the chimney breasts, the conviction that the wind itself comes only from the next street, all wedge together to keep destruction out, to deflect the eye of the developer. And when destruction comes, it is total: the printed notices on the walls, block by block, a few doors left open at night, broken windows advancing down a street until fallen slates appear on the pavement and are not kicked away. Then, after a few weeks of this, the machines arrive.

The Entertainment of War

I saw the garden where my aunt had died
And her two children and a woman from next door;
It was like a burst pod filled with clay.

A mile away in the night I had heard the bombs
Sing and then burst themselves between cramped houses
With bright soft flashes and sounds like banging doors;

The last of them crushed the four bodies into the ground,
Scattered the shelter, and blasted my uncle's corpse
Over the housetop and into the street beyond.

Now the garden lay stripped and stale; the iron shelter
Spread out its separate petals around a smooth clay saucer,
Small, and so tidy it seemed nobody had ever been there.

When I saw it, the house was blown clean by blast and care:
Relations had already torn out the new fireplaces;
My cousin's pencils lasted me several years.

And in his office notepad that was given me
I found solemn drawings in crayon of blondes without dresses;
In his lifetime I had not known him well.

These were the things I noticed at ten years of age;
Those, and the four hearses outside our house,
The chocolate cakes, and my classmates' half-shocked envy.

But my grandfather went home from the mortuary
And for five years tried to share the noises in his skull;
Then he walked out and lay under a furze-bush to die.

When he came home from identifying the daughter
My father had asked us to remind him of her mouth.
We tried. He said 'I think it was the one'.

These were marginal people whom I had met only rarely,
And the end of the whole household meant that no grief was seen;
Never have people seemed so absent from their own deaths.

This bloody episode of four whom I could understand better dead
Gave me something I needed to keep a long story moving;
I had no pain of it; can find no scar even now.

But had my belief in the fiction of war not been thus buoyed up
I might, in the sigh and strike of the next night's bombs
Have realised a little what they meant, and for the first time been afraid.

North Area

Those whom I love avoid all mention of it,
Though certain gestures they've in common
Persuade me they know it well;
A place where I can never go.

No point in asking why, or why not.
I picture it, though –
There must be dunes with cement walks,
A twilight of aluminium
Among beach huts and weather-stained handrails,
Much glass to reflect the clouds;
And a glint of blood in the cat-ice that holds the rushes.

The edge of the city. A low hill with houses on one side and rough common land and on the other, stretching down to where a dye-works lies along the valley road. Pithead gears thrust out above the hawthorn bushes; everywhere pre-fabricated workshops jut into the fields and the allotments. The society of singing birds and the society of mechanical hammers inhabit the world together, slightly ruffled and confined by each other's presence.

By the Pond

This is bitter enough: the pallid water
With yellow rushes crowding toward the shore,
The fishermen's shack,

The Pit-mound's taut and staring new wire fences,
The ashen sky. All these can serve as conscience;
For the rest, I'll live.

*

At the time when the great streets were carelessly and, it
now seems, effortlessly, thrust out along the ancient high-
roads and trackways, the tall houses shouldering solidly
towards the country and the back streets filling in the
widening spaces between them like webbed membranes,
the power of will in the town was more openly confident,
less speciously democratic, than it is now. There were, of
course, cottage railway stations, a jail that pretended to be
a castle out of Grimm, public urinals surrounded by screens
of cast-iron lacework painted green and scarlet; but there
was also an arrogant and ponderous architecture that dwarfed
and terrified the people by its sheer size and functional
brutality: the workhouses and the older hospitals, the thick-
walled abattoir, the long vaulted market-halls, the striding
canal bridges and railway viaducts. Brunel was welcome
here. Compared with these structures the straight white
blocks and concrete roadways of today are a fairground, a
clear dream just before waking, the creation of salesmen
rather than of engineers. The new city is bred out of a
hard will, but as it appears, it shows itself a little ingratiating,

a place of arcades, passages, easy ascents, good light. The eyes twinkle, beseech and veil themselves; the full, hard mouth, the broad jaw – these are no longer made visible to all.

*

A hundred years ago this was the edge of town. The goods yards, the gasworks and the coal stores were established on tips and hillocks in the sparse fields that lay among the thinning houses. Between this place and the centre, a mile or two away up the hill, lay a continuous huddle of low streets and courts, filling the marshy valley of the meagre river that now flows in a culvert under the brick and tarmac. The two main lines came curving in round the hill which confronts the town across the valley. Then they had to leap. The feet of the viaducts were planted down among the streets. One of the tracks was soon taken across into the hillside, tunnelling under the main streets and coming out at the other edge: the other stopped as soon as it reached the rising slope. A great station was built, towering, stucco-fronted, stony. The sky above it was southerly. The stately approach, the long curves of yellow wall, still remain, but the place is a goods depot with most of its doors barred and homely pots of geraniums at those windows that are not shuttered. You come upon it suddenly in its open prospect out of tangled streets of small factories. It draws light to itself, especially at sunset, standing still and smooth faced, looking westwards up the hill. Yet I am not able to imagine the activity that must once have been here. I can see no ghosts of men and women, only the gigantic ghost of stone. They are too frightened of it to pull it down.

Toyland

Today the sunlight is the paint on lead soldiers
Only they are people scattering out of the cool church

And as they go across the gravel and among the spring streets
They spread formality: they know, we know, what they have been doing

The old couples, the widowed, the staunch smilers,
The deprived and the few nubile young lily-ladies

And we know what they will do when they have opened the doors of
                                    their houses and walked in:
Mostly they will make water, and wash their calm hands and eat.

The organ's flourishes finish; the verger closes the doors;
The choirboys run home, and the rector goes off in his motor.

Here a policeman stalks, with the sun glinting on his helmet-crest;
Then a man pushes a perambulator home; and somebody posts a letter.

If I sit here long enough, loving it all, I shall see the District Nurse
                                    pedal past,
The children going to Sunday School and the strollers strolling.

The lights darting on in different rooms as night comes in;
And I shall see washing hung out, and the postman delivering letters.

I might by exception see an ambulance or the fire brigade
Or even, if the chance came round, street musicians (singing and playing)

For the people I've seen, this is the operation of life:
I need the paint of stillness and sunshine to see it that way.

The secret laugh of the world picks them up and shakes them like
peas boiling;
They behave as if nothing had happened; maybe they no longer notice.

I notice: I laugh with the laugh, cultivate it and make much of it,
But I still don't know what the joke is, to tell them.

*

... On the station platform, near a pile of baskets, a couple
embraced, pressed close together and swaying a little. It
was hard to see where the girl's feet and legs were. The
suspicion this aroused soon caused her hands, apparently
joined behind her lover's back, to become a small brown
paper parcel under the arm of a stout engine-driver who
leaned, probably drunk, against the baskets, his cap so far
forward as almost to conceal his face. I could not banish
the thought that what I had first seen was in fact his own
androgynous fantasy, the self-sufficient core of his stupor.
Such a romantic thing, so tender, for him to contain. He
looked more comic and complaisant than the couple had
done, and more likely to fall heavily to the floor.

*

.... A café with a frosted glass door through which
much light is diffused. A tall young girl comes out and
stands in front of it, her face and figure quite obscured by
this milky radiance.

She treads out on to a lopsided ochre panel of pavement before the doorway and becomes visible as a coloured shape, moving sharply. A wrap of honey and ginger, a flared saffron skirt, grey-white shoes. She goes off past the Masonic Temple with a young man: he is pale, with dark hair and a shrunken, earnest face. You could imagine him a size larger. Just for a moment, as it happens, there is no one else in the street at all. Their significance escapes rapidly like a scent, before the footsteps vanish among the car engines.

*

One afternoon I walked along the rickety boardwalk that had replaced the pavement outside the Listowel while it was being demolished. It was narrow, bounded on one side by a yellow hoarding and on the other by iron scaffolding over which the lower edges of the canvas curtain hung. Two people could just pass. Halfway along this I found myself giving way to a tall elderly woman who stared straight ahead, softly, and made no effort to accommodate herself to the shuffling files of men and women. She was thin, and dingily dressed, and her complexion was livid, a dirty vegetable colour that I had never seen in flesh before. To walk anywhere must have been for her an effort that almost destroyed consciousness. Her neck, from the throat of the jacket to the ear, was encased in a support of plastic or leather, ridged like the tubing of an enormous gas-mask, and of a subdued, rubbed, yellowish grey. I drew back, and she passed.

Weeks later, in the shopping centre of a suburb four or five miles away, I caught a glimpse of her, similarly brief, between two vans parked across the street.

Those two moments were the same, or interchangeable. They could be piled one on the other, like pennies. To me she was horrible and fascinating but not sick in the sense that she exacted my concern. Had we met, had we then possessed any common language, I would willingly have talked to her of war, of food, of children, of death. I would not have wished to hear of the movements of her disease. Had she insisted on bringing it into the conversation, I would have felt obliged to mention my own disease, which is hereditary, complete in its domination of me, progressive, so slow as to be barely perceptible. But as I saw her, knowing nothing except what I saw, the two moments were the same; as there were two, I had to pile them.

*

A man in the police court. He looked dapper and poker-faced, his arms straight, the long fingers just touching the hem of his checked jacket. Four days after being released from the prison where he had served two years for theft he had been discovered at midnight clinging like a tree-shrew to the bars of a glass factory-roof. He made no attempt to explain his presence there; the luminous nerves that made him fly up to it were not visible in daylight, and the police seemed hardly able to believe this was the creature they had brought down in the darkness.

If I could climb on the slate roof of this house now I could see the towers of the jail where he is.

In this city the governing authority is limited and mean: so limited that it can do no more than preserve a superficial order. It supplies fuel, water and power. It removes a fair proportion of the refuse, cleans the streets after a fashion, and discourages fighting. With these few things it is content. This could never be a capital city for all its size. There is no mind in it, no regard. The sensitive, the tasteful, the fashionable, the intolerant and powerful, have not moved through it as they have moved through London, evaluating it, altering deliberately, setting in motion wars of feeling about it. Most of it has never been seen.

*

In an afternoon of dazzling sunlight in the thronged streets, I saw at first no individuals but a composite monster, its unfeeling surfaces matted with dust: a mass of necks, limbs without extremities, trunks without heads; unformed stirrings and shovings spilling across the streets it had managed to get itself provided with.

Later, as the air cooled, flowing loosely about the buildings that stood starkly among the declining rays, the creature began to divide and multiply. At crossings I could see people made of straws, rags, cartons, the stuffing of burst cushions, kitchen refuse. Outside the Grand Hotel, a long-boned, carrot-haired girl with glasses, loping along, with strips of bright colour, rich, silky green and blue, in her soft clothes. For a person made of such scraps she was beautiful.

Faint blue light dropping down through the sparse leaves of the plane trees in the churchyard opposite after sundown, cooling and shaping heads, awakening eyes.

The Judgment

At the entrance to the subway,
Sensing the thud of coins
In his tray of shoelaces,

The motionless blind beggar,
Accustomed to the crowd,
Its clatter and exhalation,

Listens no more for voices,
But concentrates all day
On private sounds from a portable radio.

The Hill behind the Town

Sullen hot noon, a loop of wire,
With zinc light standing everywhere;
    A glint on the chapels,
    Glint on the chapels.

Under my heel, a loop of wire
Dragged in the dust is earth's wide eye;
    Unseen for days,
    Unseen days.

Geranium-wattled, fenced in wire,
Caged white cockerels crowd near
    And stretch red throats,
    Stretch red throats;

Their cries tear grievous through taut wire,
Drowned in tanks of factory sirens
  At sullen noon,
  Sullen hot noon.

The day's on end; a loop of wire
Kicked from the dust's bleak daylight leaves
  A blind white world,
  Blind white world.

The Poplars

Where the road divides
    Just out of town
   By the wall beyond the filling-station
Four lombardy poplars
Brush stiff against the moorland wind.

Clarity is in their tops
   That no one can touch
    Till they are dead and brushwood:

To know these tall pointers
    I need to withdraw
   From what is called my life
And from my net
   Of achievable desires.

Why should their rude and permanent virginity
So capture me? Why should studying
             These lacunae of possibility
        Relax the iron templates of obligation
Leaving me simply Man?

All I have done, or can do
Is prisoned in its act:

I think I am afraid of becoming
A cemetery of performance.

Starting to Make a Tree

First we carried out the faggot of steel stakes; they varied
in length, though most were taller than a man.

We slid one free of the bundle and drove it into the ground,
first padding the top with rag, that the branch might not
be injured with leaning on it.

Then we took turns to choose stakes of the length we
wanted, and to feel for the distances between them. We
gathered to thrust them firmly in.

There were twenty or thirty of them in all; and when they
were in place we had, round the clearing we had left for
the trunk, an irregular radial plantation of these props,

each with its wad of white at the tip. It was to be an old, down-curving tree.

This was in keeping with the burnt, chemical blue of the soil, and the even hue of the sky which seemed to have been washed with a pale brownish smoke;

another clue was the flatness of the horizon on all sides except the north, where it was broken by the low slate or tarred shingle roofs of the houses, which stretched away from us for a mile or more.

This was the work of the morning. It was done with care, for we had no wish to make revisions;

we were, nonetheless, a little excited, and hindered the women at their cooking in our anxiety to know whose armpit and whose groin would help us most in the modelling of the bole, and the thrust of the boughs.

That done, we spent the early dusk of the afternoon gathering materials from the nearest houses; and there was plenty:

a great flock mattress; two carved chairs; cement; chicken-wire; tarpaulin; a smashed barrel; lead piping; leather of all kinds; and many small things.

In the evening we sat late, and discussed how we could best use them. Our tree was to be very beautiful.

*

Coda

Yet whenever I am forced to realise that some of these people around me, people I have actually seen, whose hopeful and distended surface I have at moments touched, are bodily in love and express that love bodily to dying-point, I feel that it is my own energy, my own hope, tension and sense of time in hand, that have gathered and vanished down that dark drain; that it is I who am left, shivering and exhausted, to try and kick the lid back into place so that I can go on without the fear. And the terror that fills that moment or hour while I do it is a terror of anaesthesia: being able to feel only vertically, like a blind wall, or thickly, like the tyres of a bus.

Lovers turn to me faces of innocence where I would rather see faces of bright cunning. They have disappeared for entire hours into the lit holes of life, instead of lying stunned on its surface as I, and so many, do for so long; or instead of raising their heads cautiously and scenting the manifold airs that blow through the streets. Sex fuses the intersections of the web where it occurs into blobs that drag and stick; and the web is not meant to stand such weights. Often there is no web.

*

Once I wanted to prove the world was sick. Now I want to prove it healthy. The detection of sickness means that death has established itself as an element of the timetable; it has come within the range of the measurable. Where there is no time there is no sickness.

*

Sitting in the dark, I see a window, a large sash window of four panes, such as might be found in the living-room of any fair-sized old house. Its curtains are drawn back and it looks out on to a small damp garden, narrow close at hand where the kitchen and outhouses lead back, and then almost square. It is surrounded by privet and box, and the flowerbeds are empty save for a few laurels or rhododendrons, some leafless rose shrubs and a giant yucca. It is a December afternoon, and it is raining. Not far from the window is a black marble statue of a long-haired, long-bearded old man. His robes are conventionally archaic, and he sits, easily enough, on what seems a pile of small boulders, staring intently and with a look of great intelligence towards the patch of wall just under the kitchen window. The statue looks grimy, but its exposed surfaces are highly polished by the rain, so that the nose and the cheekbones stand out strongly on the gloom. It is rather smaller than life-size. It is clearly not in its proper place; resting as it does across the moss of the raised border, it is appreciably tilted forward and to one side, almost as if it had been abandoned as too heavy by those who were trying to move it – either in or out.

The Wind at Night

The suburb lies like a hand tonight,
A man's thick hand, so stubborn
No child or poet can move it.

The wind drives itself mad with messages,
Clattering train wheels over the roofs,
Collapsing streets of sound until
Far towers, daubed with swollen light,
Lunge closer to abuse it,

This suburb like a sleeping hand,
With helpless elms that shudder
Angry between its fingers,
Powerless to disprove it.

And, love, although the wind derides
The spaces of this stupid quarter,
And sets the time of night on edge,
It mocks the hand, but cannot lose it:

This stillness keeps us in the flesh,
For us to use it.

Do Not Remain Too Much Alone

There was a hole in the floorboards;
    I called it poetry
Because it covered a void,
    A dusty mystery,
And also because it had
    An orifice of form
Whose draught about my bed
    Kept me from lying warm.

I gazed at it for days,
    Ran my fingers round,
Whistled in it, and made
    A hoarse, sad sound;
Then I resolved to fill it,
    And scorning putty or glue
Fashioned a bread pellet,
    But it fell through.

So did the rest likewise
    Till all my loaf was gone,
And the thought of it lying there
    Set me thinking on
The need for filling with sand
    The whole capacious tunnel,
Pinch by pinch from my fingers
    Or through a funnel.

This kept me busy through
   Seasons beyond measure
And watching the grains cascade
   Gave me much pleasure
Until, disheartened by
   The way success receded,
I said variety
   Was what we both needed.

I prodded lengths of string
   Down with a long pin,
I fetched water and milk
   And let them trickle in;
Lead shot, nail pairings, currants,
   Torn–up paper bags,
Splinters that once were furniture
   And my clothes cut into rags;

And so, morsel by morsel,
   Till its last trick was sprung
I poked my life away into
   The bland English tongue.

(– Chorus: –

      'O once I went a courting
        of a girl called Mary May;
      But I poked my life away boys,
        I poked my life away'

(diminuendo: cheek against urinal floor: –

I poked my life

I poked my life

I poked my

life

away ...)

Then Hallucinations

City II

(1962)

Thinking back to the yard of Maclean, the tombstone maker, I find strange new arrivals there. Four things. Greyish-white, corpse-colour. Indeed, the most arresting of them is the figure of a woman, quite nude, lying stiffly on her side on the gravel between the polished headstones, looking as if she had been tipped there after the limbs had grown rigid. The others are what appears to be an albino raven lying similarly, with folded wings; a neat pile of coke ash and clinker; and a man's cotton singlet, clean but frayed into holes at the hem. This vest is as such a garment might be, soft and light; the wind flutters it where it lies draped. The ashes too are visibly loose and of a natural texture, though somewhat bleached. But the woman and the bird seem stony hard, like waxworks or petrified things.

The woman is tall and lean, not beautiful. A flat narrow belly, breasts that are hardly noticeable; a stringy, athletic physique. The shoulders are high and square, the face supercilious and a little mean, with a nose that curves strongly over a long upper lip and a poor chin. There is no expression and the eyes are shut as in an unguarded sleep. The hair, quite fair and straight, is fastened close to the head in a kind of plait, such as sternly reared little girls might wear. It is a body that has been put under strain by the will.

The bird – I do not know so much about birds: it may be a jackdaw, not a raven. It is quite large, with ragged feathers and knobbly claws. But it has a great smoothness and dignity in its lack of colour; the beak and eyes are lightly closed and the head inclined a little forwards. This is the least welcome of the four.

The ashes make a roughly conical pile six or eight inches high. They seem to be the product of an unusual heat.

Some marble chippings have got in amongst them, and there are faint gleams from streaks of fused metal.

As for the vest, it is exactly the sort of undergarment I have worn in winter through most of my life; though it is clearly of a small size. Cheap in the first place, and now obviously worn to a state where it would be too thin for warmth and too ragged for comfort.

*

The city asleep. In it there are shadows that are sulphurous, like tanks of black bile. The glitter on the roadways is the deceptive ore that shines on coal.

Silvered rails that guide pedestrians at street corners stand useless. Towards midnight, or at whatever hour the sky descends with its full iron weight, the ceilings drop lower everywhere; each light is partial, and proper only to its place. There is no longer any general light, only particular lights that overlap.

Out of the swarming thoroughfares, the night makes its own streets with a rake that drags persuaded people out of its way: streets where the greater buildings have already swung themselves round to odd angles against the weakened currents of the traffic.

There are lamplit streets where the full darkness is only in the deep drains and in the closed eyesockets and shut throats of the old as they lie asleep; their breath moves red tunnel-lights in their nostrils.

The arterial highways hold their white-green lights with difficulty, like long, loaded boughs; when the machines stop moving down them their gradients reappear.

Journeys at night: sometimes grooves in a thick substance, sometimes raised weals on a black skin.

The city at night has no eye, any more than it has by day, although you would expect to find one; and over much of it the sleep is aqueous and incomplete, like that of a hospital ward.

But to some extent it stops, drops and congeals. It could be broken like asphalt, and the men and women rolled out like sleeping maggots.

*

The Bull of Night. I give to the night of the city a foreign image, that of a black long-horned bull, whose giant body in the sky contains us, in one of the whorls of light that mark the tips of his horns, or his eyes or his hooves. In him the city is small, tender and bright, a helpless thing, joined to him only by the sullen weight of unknown energy it holds. I can suppose that his obscure and incorporeal shape moves either among the stars or can be seen, extending beyond the scattered lights of the city that forms part of him. I can imagine his red eye goggling low in the sky or out along the railway tracks. He is the most frivolous and ancient of the gods with whom I replace the god of England: in him, some things are possible.

...... An orderly underground bar full of men, towards closing time. If I close my eyes, I move from a small, brightly-lit room of brown wood and red leather into the crazy caverns of his body. Into a world of spaciousness, and of deep sound that comes in several suggested dimensions. No sight, except a sense of epic underground light on my eyelids. Then odours come, and I am fetched off into memory: memories not of actual things but of imagined ones; or at times I feel that what I am imagining is masquerading as memory. Great wakefulness and pleasure of the senses.

I see beasts trundling along among railway wagons in the fog, with coloured lamps in their heads. A furnace door opens and a blast of voices comes out with the glare. There are gantries and jibs that climb up among one another's girders, threaded with globular lights that glow, bobbing, in the dusk.

I feel my fingers numb with thought. My mind tunes itself approximately to a pitch-level and hears certain sliding sequences of tones, rising and falling seconds, eddying gradually up and down like drunken songs, as the various speaking voices in the room strike the tones in passing. The sequences of voices have a pattern, a long shallow curve, shaped like the arc of a gong. Over the top of this hollow copper music a sudden whistle hops up and down like a paper bird.

I have no sense of walls. The limit of the world is smoke, rolling in the distance, trailing between the horns of the bull.

*

Walking through the suburb at night, as I pass the dentist's house I hear a clock chime a quarter, a desolate brassy sound. I know where it stands, on the mantelpiece in the still surgery. The chime falls back into the house, and beyond it, without end. Peace.

I sense the simple nakedness of these tiers of sleeping men and women beneath whose windows I pass. I imagine it in its own setting, a mean bathroom in a house no longer new, a bathroom with plank panelling, painted a peculiar shade of green by an amateur, and badly preserved. It is full of steam, so much as to obscure the yellow light and hide the high, patched ceiling. In this dream, standing quiet, the private image of a householder or his wife, damp and clean.

I see this as it might be floating in the dark, as if the twinkling point of a distant streetlamp had blown in closer, swelling and softening to a foggy oval. I can call up a series of such glimpses that need have no end, for they are all the bodies of strangers. Some are deformed or diseased, some are ashamed, but the peace of humility and weakness is there in them all. The story they tell is an old one.

I have often felt myself to be vicious, in living so much by the eye, yet among so many people. I can be afraid that the egg of light through which I see these bodies might present itself as a keyhole. Yet I can find no sadism in the way I see them now. They are warm-fleshed, yet their shapes have the minuscule, remote morality of some mediaeval woodcut of the Expulsion: an eternally startled Adam, a permanently bemused Eve. I see them as homunculi, moving privately each in a softly lit fruit in a nocturnal tree. I can consider without scorn or envy the well-found bedrooms I pass, walnut and rosepink, altars of tidy, dark-haired women, bare-backed, wifely. Even in these I can see order.

*

...... I come quite often now upon a sort of ecstasy, a rag of light blowing among the things I know, making me feel I am not the one for whom it was intended, that I have inadvertently been looking through another's eyes and have seen what I cannot receive......

*

'And I have seen the spots of blood on the soft feathers of its wings,' I once said that about this place. And I have thought of those wings as the wings of a gull that might come here in winter, flapping in from the coast a hundred miles away, congregating with others on green playing fields and the untended recesses of parks in the suburbs; I have thought of them as the wings of a pigeon awake, bleak-eyed, before the human dawn, a bird from one of those flocks that wheel dazzling above the crowded roofs; I have thought of them as the wings of a dove, that has no place here.

My bird, my unwelcome albino raven that has appeared at last, is not one of the city's living birds: sparrows, starlings, pigeons, a few thrushes and blackbirds on the outskirts, robins in the larger gardens, are all we have – and the fanciful waterfowl on the park ponds. Yet this petrified freak is the bird of my city, my bird for this place. It would not have come to me anywhere else.

The city could have produced it from within itself; it is spacious enough, secret enough. There are suburbs I have never properly visited, or have never managed to find recognisable as I have passed through them, districts that melt into one another without climax. In one of these in a side road out of a side road, this bird might have been bred and manufactured, in a large shed running the whole length of a garden that is cut off by the high wall of an old timberyard or repair shop. By whom? a small family business in the last stages of decay: the father, sixty, short and quick, with baggy overalls, a scrawny, mobile neck, a small round head with stiff grey hair brushed upwards even at the back, and little fat lips. The son, nearly thirty, just married; taller than the father, but similar, with a weaker neck and hollower cheeks. His hair is fair, like the brows and lashes of his singularly puffy eyes. The uncle, in his fifties, and unmarried, is crablike and stout with a lined reddish face and very dark hair, quite wavy.

It is possible that they supply pet-shops; or maybe they make garden ornaments of cement or creosoted logs, bird-tables, rustic seats, gnomes, rabbits, toadstools. In some crisis or exultation, or exhaustion, lost for a while to the sense of the world, they may have produced my bird without realising it.

What is it? Napoleon. Goethe. A stillborn ruler for the city. Cold, large-headed, enormously wise, completely immobile.

It is important that it was born through these people, or through me, without any sort of Annunciation. Anything that is publicly announced is rapidly destroyed by the million familiar little glances of the people. The things that are themselves, that go to make the body of the city, are unannounced, are made without full consultation or advice, without consideration for feeling. The new buildings are part of that body for the moment, while they are incomplete, because the power that raises them is a force of such complete and unscrupulous cupidity that the press has no vocabulary for describing it. Financially, it is possible that the work might be brought to a standstill and never continued; the town might be left half-disembowelled, a possibility so monstrous that no one considers it. And the speculators go on gambling.

The bird is the poetry of the city that nobody has ever dared speak. The poetry of the unseen colossus that lies hidden among countless lights. It is unwelcome in the same way that tea-leaves in a cup are unwelcome; it has a similar flavour of bitterness, origin and command. I resent its inscrutability, the suspicion I have that it may be worthless, the doubts I have about whether it is moral or sensual. It reveals no taste whatever. In that, certainly, it is like a part of the natural world. I thought at first that it was so obviously literary, so hoarily embedded in the symbolism of the last century, that I could account it an aberration and so dismiss it, but its urbane banality is clearly something I must have been desiring. With the other three things only, I should have been too comfortable, and too lonely: a woman, a heap of ashes, a vest – I could have been a Crusoe within myself. Slowly this bird and I are working on each other. The only rule in our game is that neither of us must appear to change.

*

I want to believe I live in a single world. That is why I am keeping my eyes at home while I can. The light keeps on separating the world like a table knife: it sweeps across what I see and suggests what I do not. The imaginary comes to me with as much force as the real, the remembered with as much force as the immediate. The countries on the map divide and pile up like ice-floes. What is strange is that I feel no stress, no grating discomfort among this confusion, no loss; only a belief that I should not be here. I see the iron fences and the shallow ditches of the countryside the mild wind has travelled over. I cannot enter that countryside; nor can I escape it. I cannot join together the mild wind and the shallow ditches, I cannot lay the light across the world and then watch it slide away. Each thought is at once translucent and icily capricious. A polytheism without gods.

*

Good times? Yes, there have been good times: without them there would be no city, only a flat hell-town, excremental, littered with malice, obstruction and failure. I am talking about a place to live, and the way of it. You know about your pleasures – and I don't mention them, in case my words should turn into priests.

This city is like the Bride of Marcel Duchamp; and when she is stripped the Glass needs to be broken and carted away.

CITY

(Roy Fisher typescript, *c.* 1962-63)

On one of the steep slopes that rise towards the centre of the city all the buildings have been destroyed within the past year: a whole district of the tall narrow houses that spilled around what were a hundred years ago outlying factories has gone. The streets remain, among the rough quadrilaterals of brick rubble, veering awkwardly towards one another through nothing; at night their rounded surfaces still shine under the irregularly-set gaslamps, and tonight they dully reflect also the yellowish flare, diffused and baleful, that hangs flat in the clouds a few hundred feet above the city's invisible heart. Occasional cars move cautiously across this waste, as if suspicious of the emptiness; there is little to separate the roadways from what lies between them. Their tail-lights vanish slowly into the blocks of surrounding buildings, maybe a quarter of a mile from the middle of the desolation.

And what is it that lies between these purposeless streets? There is not a whole brick, a foundation to stumble across, a drainpipe, a smashed fowlhouse; the entire place has been razed flat, dug over, and smoothed down again. The bald curve of the hillside shows quite clearly here, near its crown, where the brilliant road, stacked close on either side with warehouses and shops, runs out towards the west. Down below, the district that fills the hollow is impenetrably black. The streets there are so close and so twisted among their massive tenements that it is impossible to trace the line of a single one of them by its lights. The lamps that can be seen shine oddly, and at mysterious distances, as if they were in a marsh. Only the great flat-roofed factory shows clear by its bulk, stretching across three or four whole blocks just below the edge of the waste, with solid rows of lit windows.

Lullaby and Exhortation for the Unwilling Hero

A fish,
Firelight,
A watery ceiling:
Under the door
The drunk wind sleeps.

The bell in the river,
The loaf half eaten,
The coat of the sky.

A pear,
Perfume,
A white glade of curtains:
Out in the moonlight
The smoke reaches high.

The statue in the cellar,
The skirt on the chairback,
The throat of the street.

A shell,
Shadow,
A floor spread with silence:
Faint on the skylight
The fat moths beat.

The pearl in the stocking,
The coals left to die,
The bell in the river,

CITY: TYPESCRIPT (*c.* 1962-63)

The loaf half eaten,
The coat of the sky.

The night slides like a thaw
And oil drums bang together.

A frosted-glass door opening, then another.
Orange and blue decor.
The smoke that hugs the ceiling tastes of pepper.

What steps descend, what rails conduct?
Sodium bulbs equivocate,
And cowls of ventilators
With limewashed breath hint at the places
To which the void lift cages plunge or soar.

Prints on the landing walls
Are all gone blind with steam;
A voice under the floor
Swings a dull axe against a door.

The gaping office block of night
Shudders into the deep sky overhead:

Thrust down your foot in sleep
Among its depths. Do not respect
The janitors in bed,
The balustrades of iron bars,
The gusty stairwells; thrust it deep,
Into a concrete garage out of sight,
And rest among the cars
That, shut in filtered moonlight,
Sweat mercury and lead.

Subway trains, or winds of indigo,
Bang oil-drums in the yard for war:
Already, half-built towers
Over the bombed city
Show mouths that soon will speak no more,
Stoppered with the perfections of tomorrow.

You can lie women in your bed
With glass and mortar in their hair.
Pocket the key, and draw the curtains,
They'll not care.

Letters on a sweetshop window:
At last the rain slides them askew,
The foetus in the dustbin moves one claw.

And from the locomotive
That's halted on the viaduct
A last white rag of steam
Blows ghostly across the gardens.
When you wake, what will you do?

Under the floorboards of your dream
Gun barrels rolled in lint
Jockey the rooms this way and that.
Across the suburbs, squares of colour gleam:
Swaddled in pink and apricot,
The people are 'making love'.

Those are bright points that flicker
Softly, and vanish one by one.
Your telegraphic fingers mutter the world.
What will they reach for when your sleep is done?

CITY: TYPESCRIPT (*c.* 1962-63)

The hiss of tyres along the gutter,
Odours of polish in the air;
A car sleeps in the neighbouring room,
A wardrobe by its radiator.

The rumbling canisters beat for you
Who are a room now altogether bare,
An open mouth pressed outwards against life,
Tasting the sleepers' breath,
The palms of hands, discarded shoes,
Lilac wood, the blade of a breadknife.

Before dawn in the sidings,
Over whose even tracks
Fat cooling towers caress the sky,
The rows of trucks
Extend: black, white,
White, grey, white, black,
Black, white, black, grey,

Marshalled like building blocks:

Women are never far away.

In the century that has passed since this city has become great, it has twice laid itself out in the shape of a wheel. The ghost of the older one still lies among the spokes of the new, those dozen highways that thread constricted ways through the inner suburbs, then thrust out, twice as wide, across the housing estates and into the countryside, dragging moraines of buildings with them. Sixty or seventy years ago there were other main roads, quite as important as these were then, but lying between their paths. By day they are simply alternatives, short cuts, lined solidly with parked cars and crammed with delivery vans. They look merely like side-streets, heartlessly overblown in some excess of Victorian expansion. By night, or on a Sunday, you can see them for what they are. They are still lit meagrely, and the long rows of houses, three and four storeys high, rear black above the lamps enclosing the roadways, clamping them off from whatever surrounds them. From these pavements you can sometimes see the sky at night, not obscured as it is in most parts of the city by the greenish-blue haze of light that steams out of the mercury vapour lamps. These streets are not worth lighting. The houses have not been turned into shops – they are not villas either that might have become offices, but simply tall dwellings, opening straight off the street, with cavernous entries leading into back courts.

The people who live in them are mostly very old. Some have lived through three wars, some through only one; wars of newspapers, of mysterious sciences, of coercion, of disappearance. Wars that have come down the streets from the unknown city and the unknown world, like rainwater floods in the gutters. There are small shops at street corners, with faceless rows of houses between them; and taverns carved only shallowly into the massive walls. When these people go into the town, the buses they travel in stop just before they reach it, in the sombre back streets behind the Town Hall and the great insurance offices.

These lost streets are decaying only very slowly. The

impacted lives of their inhabitants, the meaninglessness of news, the dead black of the chimney breasts, the conviction that the wind itself comes only from the next street, all wedge together to keep destruction out, to deflect the eye of the developer. And when destruction comes, it is total: the printed notices on the walls, block by block, a few doors left open at night, broken windows advancing down a street until fallen slates appear on the pavement and are not kicked away. Then, after a few weeks of this, the machines arrive.

The Entertainment of War

I saw the garden where my aunt had died
And her two children and a woman from next door;
It was like a burst pod filled with clay.

A mile away in the night I had heard the bombs
Sing and then burst themselves between cramped houses
With bright soft flashes and sounds like banging doors;

The last of them crushed the four bodies into the ground,
Scattered the shelter, and blasted my uncle's corpse
Over the housetop and into the street beyond.

Now the garden lay stripped and stale; the iron shelter
Spread out its separate petals around a smooth clay saucer,
Small, and so tidy it seemed nobody had ever been there.

When I saw it, the house was blown clean by blast and care:
Relations had already torn out the new fireplaces;
My cousin's pencils lasted me several years.

And in his office notepad that was given me
I found solemn drawings in crayon of blondes without dresses;
In his lifetime I had not known him well.

These were the things I noticed at ten years of age;
Those, and the four hearses outside our house,
The chocolate cakes, and my classmates' half-shocked envy.

But my grandfather went home from the mortuary
And for five years tried to share the noises in his skull,
Then he walked out and lay under a furze-bush to die.

When my father came back from identifying the daughter
He asked us to remind him of her mouth.
We tried. He said 'I think it was the one.'

These were marginal people whom I had met only rarely
And the end of the whole household meant that no grief was seen;
Never have people seemed so absent from their own deaths.

This bloody episode of four whom I could understand better dead
Gave me something I needed to keep a long story moving;
I had no pain of it; can find no scar even now.

But had my belief in the fiction not been thus buoyed up
I might, in the sigh and strike of the next night's bombs
Have realised a little what they meant, and for the first time been afraid.

CITY: TYPESCRIPT (*c.* 1962-63)

North Area

Those whom I love avoid all mention of it,
Though certain gestures they've in common
Persuade me they know it well;
A place where I can never go.

No point in asking why, or why not.
I picture it, though –
There must be dunes with cement walks,
A twilight of aluminium
Among beach huts and weather-stained handrails,
Much glass to reflect the clouds;
And a glint of blood in the cat-ice that holds the rushes.

The edge of the city. A low hill with houses on one side and rough common land on the other, stretching down to where a dye-works lies along the valley road. Pithead gears thrust out above the hawthorn bushes; everywhere prefabricated workshops jut into the fields and the allotments. The society of singing birds and the society of mechanical hammers inhabit the world together, slightly ruffled and confined by each other's presence.

By the Pond

This is bitter enough: the pallid water
With yellow rushes crowding toward the shore,
That fishermen's shack.

The pit-mound's taut and staring new wire fences,
The ashen sky. All these can serve as conscience;
For the rest, I'll live.

Brick-dust in sunlight. That is what I see now in the city, a dry epic flavour, whose air is human breath. A place of walls made straight with plumbline and trowel, to desiccate and crumble in the sun and smoke. Blistered paint on cisterns and girders, cracking to show the priming. Old men spit on the paving slabs, little boys urinate; and the sun dries it as it dries out the patches of damp on plaster facings to leave misshapen stains. I look for things here that make old men and dead men seem young. Things which have escaped, the landscapes of countless childhoods. Wharves, the oldest parts of factories, tarred gable ends rearing to take the sun over lower roofs. Soot, sunlight, brick-dust; and the breath that tastes of them.

At the time when the great streets were thrust out along the ancient highroads and trackways, the houses shouldering solidly towards the country and the back streets filling in the widening spaces between them like webbed membranes, the power of will in the town was more openly confident, less speciously democratic, than it is now. There were, of course, cottage railway stations, a jail that pretended to be a castle out of Grimm, public urinals surrounded by screens of cast-iron lacework painted green and scarlet; but there was also an arrogant ponderous architecture that dwarfed and terrified the people by its sheer size and functional brutality: the workhouses and the older hospitals, the thick-walled abattoir, the long vaulted market-halls, the striding canal bridges and railway viaducts. Brunel was welcome here. Compared with these structures the straight white blocks and concrete roadways of today are a fairground, a clear dream just before waking, the creation of salesmen rather than of engineers. The new city is bred out of a hard will, but as it appears, it shows itself a little ingratiating, a place of arcades, passages, easy ascents, good light. The eyes twinkle, beseech and veil themselves; the full, hard mouth, the broad jaw – these are no longer made visible to all.

A street half a mile long with no buildings, only a continuous embankment of sickly grass along one side, with railway signals on it, and strings of trucks through whose black-spoked wheels you can see the sky; and for the whole length of the other a curving wall of bluish brick, caked with soot and thirty feet high. In it, a few wicket gates painted ochre, and fingermarked, but never open. Cobbles in the roadway.

A hundred years ago this was almost the edge of town. The goods yards, the gasworks and the coal stores were established on tips and hillocks in the sparse fields that lay among the houses. Between this place and the centre, a mile or two away up the hill, lay a continuous huddle of low streets and courts, filling the marshy valley of the meagre river that now flows under brick and tarmac. And this was as far as the railway came, at first. A great station was built, towering, stucco-fronted, stony. The sky above it was southerly. The stately approach, the long curves of wall, still remain, but the place is a goods depot with most of its doors barred and pots of geraniums at those windows that are not shuttered. You come upon it suddenly in its open prospect out of tangled streets of small factories. It draws light to itself, especially at sunset, standing still and smooth faced, looking westwards at the hill. I am not able to imagine the activity that must once have been here. I can see no ghosts of men and women, only the gigantic ghost of stone. They are too frightened of it to pull it down.

The Sun Hacks

The sun hacks at the slaughterhouse campanile,
And by the butchers' cars, packed tail-to-kerb,
Masks under white caps wake into human faces.

The river shudders as dawn drums on its culvert;
On the first bus nightworkers sleep, or stare
At hoardings that look out on yesterday.

The whale-back hill assumes its concrete city:
The white-flanked towers; the stillborn monuments;
The thousand golden offices, untenanted.

CITY: TYPESCRIPT (*c.* 1962-63)

At night on the station platform, near a pile of baskets, a couple embraced, pressed close together and swaying a little. It was hard to see where the girl's feet and legs were. The suspicion this aroused soon caused her hands, apparently joined behind her lover's back, to become a small brown paper parcel under the arm of a stout engine-driver who leaned, probably drunk, against the baskets, his cap so far forward as almost to conceal his face. I could not banish the thought that what I had first seen was in fact his own androgynous fantasy, the self-sufficient core of his stupor. Such a romantic thing, so tender, for him to contain. He looked more comic and complaisant than the couple had done, and more likely to fall heavily to the floor.

A café with a frosted glass door through which much light is diffused. A tall young girl comes out and stands in front of it, her face and figure quite obscured by this milky radiance.

She treads out on to a lopsided ochre panel of lit pavement before the doorway and becomes visible as a coloured shape, moving sharply. A wrap of honey and ginger, a flared saffron skirt, grey-white shoes. She goes off past the Masonic Temple with a young man: he is pale, with dark hair and a shrunken, earnest face. You could imagine him a size larger. Just for a moment, as it happens, there is no one else in the street at all. Their significance escapes rapidly like a scent, before the footsteps vanish among the car engines.

Night Walkers

Darkness hisses at the town-blocks' end.
     Salt-glaze of sleet
Pocks fingers, coldly grits the walks
Sprung flat, like table knives.

There's a smashed box of wind in every street,
And lamps, for startled hours,
     Wistfully guard
Behind their glistening panes shaken with blows
     The blanched gold cheeks
Of those we seek for miles, sardonically.

One afternoon I walked along the rickety boardwalk that
had replaced the pavement outside the hotel while it was
being demolished. It was narrow, bounded on one side by
a yellow hoarding and on the other by iron scaffolding
over which the lower edges of the canvas curtains hung.
Two people could just pass. Halfway along this I found
myself giving way to a tall elderly woman who stared
straight ahead, softly, and made no effort to accommodate
herself to the shuffling files of men and women. She was
thin, and dingily dressed, and her complexion was livid, a
dirty vegetable colour that I have never seen in flesh before.
Her neck, from the throat of the jacket to the ear, was
encased in a plastic support, ridged like the tubing of an
enormous gas-mask, and of a rubbed, yellowish grey. I
drew back, and she passed.

CITY: TYPESCRIPT (c. 1962-63)

Weeks later, in the shopping centre of a suburb four or five miles away, I caught a glimpse of her, between two vans parked across the street.

Those two moments were the same, or interchangeable. They could be piled one on the other, like pennies.

A man in the police court. He looked dapper and poker-faced, his arms straight, the long fingers just touching the hem of his checked jacket. Four days after being released from the prison where he had served two years for theft he had been discovered at midnight clinging like a tree-shrew to the bars of a glass factory-roof. He made no attempt to explain his presence there; the luminous nerves that made him fly up to it were not visible in daylight, and the police seemed hardly able to believe this was the creature they had brought down in the darkness.

In this city the governing authority is limited and mean: so limited that it can do no more than preserve a superficial order. It supplies fuel, water and power. It removes a fair proportion of the refuse, cleans the streets after a fashion, and discourages fighting. With these few things, and a few more of the same sort, it is content. This could never be a capital city for all its size. There is no mind in it, no regard. The sensitive, the tasteful, the fashionable, the intolerant and powerful, have not moved through it as they have moved through London, evaluating it, altering it deliberately, setting in motion wars of feeling about it. Most of it has never been seen.

In an afternoon of dazzling sunlight in the thronged streets, I saw at first no individuals but a composite monster, its unfeeling surfaces matted with dust: a mass of necks, limbs without extremities, trunks without heads; unformed stirrings and shovings spilling across the streets it had managed to get itself provided with.

Later, as the air cooled, flowing loosely about the buildings that stood starkly among the declining rays, the creature began to divide and multiply. At crossings I could see people made of straws, rags, cartons, the stuffing of burst cushions, kitchen refuse. Outside the Grand Hotel, a long-boned carrot-haired girl with glasses, loping along, and with strips of bright colour, rich, silky green and blue, in her soft clothes. For a person made of such scraps she was beautiful.

Faint blue light dropping down through the sparse leaves of the plane trees in the churchyard opposite after sundown, cooling and shaping heads, awakening eyes.

The Judgment

At the entrance to the subway,
Sensing the thud of coins
In his tray of shoelaces,

The motionless blind beggar,
Accustomed to the crowd,
Its clatter and exhalation,

CITY: TYPESCRIPT (*c.* 1962-63)

Listens no more for voices,
But concentrates all day
On private sounds from a portable radio.

The Hill behind the Town

Sullen hot noon, a loop of wire,
With zinc light standing everywhere;
    A glint on the chapels,
    Glint on the chapels.

Under my heel, a loop of wire
Dragged in the dust is earth's wide eye;
    Unseen for days,
    Unseen days.

Geranium-wattled, fenced in wire,
Caged white cockerels crowd near
    And stretch red throats,
    Stretch red throats;

Their cries tear grievous through taut wire,
Drowned in tanks of factory sirens
    At sullen noon,
    Sullen hot noon.

The day's on end; a loop of wire
Kicked from the dust's bleak daylight leaves
    A blind white world,
    Blind white world.

The Poplars

Where the road divides
        Just out of town
        By the wall beyond the filling-station
Four Lombardy poplars
Brush stiff against the moorland wind.

Clarity is in their tops
        That no one can touch
                Till they are felled,
        Brushwood to cart away:

To know these tall pointers
        I need to withdraw
        From what is called my life
And from my net
        Of achievable desires.

Why should their rude and permanent virginity
So capture me? Why should studying
        These lacunae of possibility
        Relax the iron templates of obligation
Leaving me simply Man?

All I have done, or can do
Is prisoned in its act:

I think I am afraid of becoming
A cemetery of performance.

CITY: TYPESCRIPT (*c.* 1962-63)

Starting to Make a Tree

First we carried out the faggot of steel stakes; they varied in length, though most were taller than a man.

We slid one free of the bundle and drove it into the ground, first padding the top with rag, that the branch might not be injured with leaning on it.

Then we took turns to choose stakes of the length we wanted, and to feel for the distances between them. We gathered to thrust them firmly in.

There were twenty or thirty of them in all; and when they were in place we had, round the clearing we had left for the trunk, an irregular radial plantation of these props, each with its wad of white at the tip. It was to be an old, downcurving tree.

This was in keeping with the burnt, chemical blue of the soil, and the even hue of the sky which seemed to have been washed with a pale brownish smoke;

another clue was the flatness of the horizon on all sides except the north, where it was broken by the low slate or tarred shingle roofs of the houses, which stretched away from us for a mile or more.

This was the work of the morning. It was done with care, for we had no wish to make revisions;

we were, nonetheless, a little excited, and hindered the women at their cooking in our anxiety to know whose armpit and whose groin would help us most in the modelling of the bole, and the thrust of the boughs.

That done, we spent the early dusk of the afternoon gathering materials from the nearest houses; and there was plenty:

a great flock mattress; two carved chairs; cement; chicken-wire; tarpaulin; a smashed barrel; lead piping, leather of all kinds; and many small things.

In the evening we sat late, and discussed how we could best use them. Our tree was to be very beautiful.

Yet whenever I am forced to realise that some of these people around me are bodily in love, I feel that it is my own energy, my own hope, tension and sense of time in hand, that have gathered and vanished down that dark drain; that it is I who am left, shivering and exhausted, to try and kick the lid back into place so that I can go on without the fear of being able to feel only vertically, like a blind wall, or thickly, like the tyres of a bus.

Lovers turn to me faces of innocence where I would rather see circumspection. They have disappeared for entire hours into the lit holes of life, instead of lying stunned on its surface as I, and so many, do for so long; or instead of raising their heads cautiously and scenting the manifold airs that blow through the streets.

CITY: TYPESCRIPT (*c.* 1962-63)

The city asleep. In it there are shadows that are sulphurous, like tanks of black bile. The glitter on the roadways is the deceptive ore that shines on coal.

The last buses have left the centre; the pallid faces of the crowd looked like pods, filled by a sick and gusty summer that had come too late for plenty.

Silvered rails that guide pedestrians at street corners stand useless. Towards midnight, or at whatever hour the sky descends with its full iron weight, the ceilings drop lower everywhere; each light is partial, and proper only to its place. There is no longer any general light, only particular lights that overlap.

Out of the swarming thoroughfares, the night makes its own streets with a rake that drags persuaded people out of its way: streets where the greater buildings have already swung themselves round to odd angles against the weakened currents of the traffic.

There are lamplit streets where the full darkness is only in the deep drains and in the closed eyesockets and shut throats of the old as they lie asleep; their breath moves red tunnel-lights in their nostrils.

The arterial highways hold their white-green lights with difficulty, like long, loaded boughs; when the machines stop moving down them their gradients reappear.

Journeys at night: sometimes grooves in a thick sub-stance, sometimes raised weals on a black skin.

The city at night has no eye, any more than it has by day, although you would expect to find one; and over much of it the sleep is aqueous and incomplete, like that of a hospital ward.

But to some extent it stops, drops and congeals. It could be broken like asphalt, and the men and women rolled out like sleeping maggots.

Once I wanted to prove the world was sick. Now I want to prove it healthy. The detection of sickness means that death has established itself as an element of the timetable; it has come within the range of the measurable. Where there is no time there is no sickness.

The Wind at Night

The suburb lies like a hand tonight,
A man's thick hand, so stubborn
No child or poet can move it.

The wind drives itself mad with messages,
Clattering train wheels over the roofs,
Collapsing streets of sound until
Far towers, daubed with swollen light,
Lunge closer to abuse it,

This suburb like a sleeping hand,
With helpless elms that shudder
Angry between its fingers,
Powerless to disprove it.

And, love, although the wind derides
The spaces of this stupid quarter,
And sets the time of night on edge,
It mocks the hand, but cannot lose it:

This stillness keeps us in the flesh,
For us to use it.

Sitting in the dark, I see a window, a large sash window of four panes, such as might be found in the living-room of any fair-sized old house. Its curtains are drawn back and it looks out on to a small damp garden, narrow close at hand where the kitchen and outhouses lead back, and then almost square. It is surrounded by privet and box, and the flowerbeds are empty save for a few laurels or rhododendrons, some leafless rose shrubs and a giant yucca. It is a December afternoon, and it is raining. Not far from the window is a black marble statue of a long-haired, long-bearded old man. His robes are conventionally archaic, and he sits, easily enough, on what seems a pile of small boulders, staring intently and with a look of great intelligence towards the patch of wall just under the kitchen window. The statue looks grimy, but its exposed surfaces are highly polished by the rain, so that the nose and the cheekbones stand out strongly in the gloom. It is rather smaller than life-size. It is clearly not in its proper place; resting as it does across the moss of the raised border, it is appreciably tilted forward and to one side, almost as if it had been abandoned as too heavy by those who were trying to move it – either in or out.

And there are other cold things. A bird, for instance, that I find in my thoughts quite often: it appears to be a dead or sculptured albino raven that lies on its side with folded wings as though it has been tipped out onto the ground after growing rigid in another posture. I know little about birds: it may be a jackdaw, not a raven. It is quite large, with ragged feathers and knobbly claws. But it has a great smoothness and dignity in its lack of colour;

the beak and eyes are lightly closed and the head inclined a little forwards. I do not welcome it.

Walking through the suburb at night, as I pass the dentist's house I hear a clock chime a quarter, a desolate brassy sound. I know where it stands, on the mantelpiece in the still surgery. The chime falls back into the house, and beyond it, without end. Peace.

I sense the simple nakedness of these tiers of sleeping men and women beneath whose windows I pass. I imagine it in its own setting, a mean bathroom in a house no longer new, a bathroom with plank panelling, painted a peculiar shade of green by an amateur, and badly preserved. It is full of steam, so much as to obscure the yellow light and hide the high, patched ceiling. In this dream, standing quiet, the private image of a householder or his wife, damp and clean.

I see this as it might be floating in the dark, as if the twinkling point of a distant streetlamp had blown in closer, swelling and softening to a foggy oval. I can call up a series of such glimpses that need have no end, for they are all the bodies of strangers. Some are deformed or diseased, some are ashamed, but the peace of humility and weakness is there in them all. The story they tell is an old one.

I have often felt myself to be vicious, in living so much by the eye, yet among so many people. I can be afraid that the egg of light through which I see these bodies might present itself as a keyhole. Yet I can find no sadism in the way I see them now. They are warmfleshed, yet their shapes have the minuscule, remote morality of some mediaeval woodcut of the Expulsion: an eternally startled Adam, a permanently bemused Eve. I see them as homunculi, moving privately each in a softly lit fruit in a nocturnal tree. I can consider without scorn or envy the well-found bedrooms I pass, walnut and rosepink, altars of tidy, dark-haired women, bare-backed, wifely. Even in these I can see order.

I come quite often now upon a sort of ecstasy, a rag of light blowing among the things I know, making me feel I am not the one for whom it was intended, that I have inadvertently been looking through another's eyes and have seen what I cannot receive.

My bird, my unwelcome albino raven that has appeared at last, is not one of the city's living birds; yet this petrified freak is my bird for this place. The city could have produced it from within itself; it is spacious enough, secret enough. There are suburbs I have never properly visited, or have never managed to find recognisable as I have passed through them, districts that melt into one another without climax. In one of these, in a side road out of a side road, this bird might have been bred and manufactured, in a large shed running the whole length of a garden that is cut off by the high wall of an old timber yard or repair shop. By whom? A small family business in the last stages of decay: the father, the most confused son, the least responsible uncle. The father, sixty, short and quick, with baggy overalls, a scrawny mobile neck, a small round head with stiff grey hair brushed upwards even at the back, and little fat lips. The son, nearly thirty, just married; taller than the father, but similar, with a weaker neck and hollower cheeks. His hair is fair, like the brows and lashes of his singularly puffy eyes. The uncle, in his fifties and unmarried, is crablike and stout with a lined reddish face and very dark hair, quite wavy.

It is possible that they supply a pet-shop; or maybe they make garden ornaments of cement or creosoted logs, bird-tables, rustic seats, gnomes, rabbits, toadstools. In some crisis or exultation, lost for a while to the sense of the world, they may have produced my bird without realising it.

What is it? Napoleon. Goethe. Cold, large-headed, enormously wise, completely immobile.

It is important that it was born, through these people or through me, without any sort of Annunciation. Anything that is publicly announced is rapidly destroyed by a million familiar little glances. The things that go to make the body of the city are unannounced, are made without full consultation or advice, without consideration for feelings. The new buildings are part of that body for the moment, while they are uncomplete, because the power that raises them is a force of such complete and unscrupulous cupidity that the press has no vocabulary for describing it. Financially it is possible that the work might be brought to a standstill and never continued; the town might be left half-disembowelled, a possibility so monstrous that nobody considers it. And the speculators go on gambling.

The bird is as unwelcome as tea-leaves in a cup are: with a flavour of bitterness, origin and command. I resent its inscrutability, the suspicion I have that it may be worthless, the doubts I have about whether it is moral or sensual. It reveals no taste whatever. In that, certainly, it is like a part of the natural world. I thought at first that it was so obviously literary, so hoarily embedded in the symbolism of the last century, that I could account it an aberration and so dismiss it, but its urbane banality is clearly something I must have been desiring. This bird and I are going to work on each other. The only rule in our game is that neither of us must appear to change.

I want to believe I live in a single world. That is why I am keeping my eyes at home while I can. The light keeps on separating the world like a table knife: it sweeps across what I see and suggests what I do not. The imaginary comes to me with as much force as the real, the remembered with as much force as the immediate. The countries on the map divide and pile up like ice-floes. What is strange is that I feel no stress, no grating discomfort among the confusion, no loss; only a belief that I should not be here. I see the iron fences and the shallow ditches of the countryside the mild wind has travelled over. I cannot enter that countryside; nor can I escape it. I cannot join together the mild wind and the shallow ditches, I cannot lay the light across the world and then watch it slide away. Each thought is at once translucent and icily capricious. A polytheism without gods.

The Park

If you should go there on such a day –
  The red sun disappearing,
  Netted behind black sycamores;

If you should go there on such a day –
  The sky drawn thin with frost,
  Its cloud-rims bright and bitter –

If you should go there on such a day,
Maybe the old goose will chase you away.

If you should go there to see
  The shallow concrete lake,
  Scummed over, fouled with paper;

If you should go there to see
  The grass plots, featureless,
  Muddy, and bruised, and balding –

If you should go there to see,
Maybe the old goose will scare you as he scared me,

Waddling fast on his diseased feet,
  His orange bill thrust out,
  His eyes indignant;

Waddling fast on his diseased feet,
  His once-ornamental feathers
  Baggy, and smeared with winter –

         CITY: TYPESCRIPT (*c.* 1962-63)

Waddling fast on his diseased feet,
The old goose will one day reach death; and be unfit to eat.

And when the goose is dead, then we
     Can say we're able, at last,
     No longer hindered from going;

And when the goose is dead, then we
     Have the chance, if we still want it,
     To wander the park at leisure;

– Oh, when excuse is dead, then we
Must visit there, most diligently.

CITY

(1969)

On one of the steep slopes that rise towards the centre of the city all the buildings have been destroyed within the past year: a whole district of the tall narrow houses that spilled around what were a hundred years ago outlying factories has gone. The streets remain, among the rough quadrilaterals of brick rubble, veering awkwardly towards one another through nothing; at night their rounded surfaces still shine under the irregularly-set gaslamps, and tonight they dully reflect also the yellowish flare, diffused and baleful, that hangs flat in the clouds a few hundred feet above the city's invisible heart. Occasional cars move cautiously across this waste, as if suspicious of the emptiness; there is little to separate the roadways from what lies between them. Their tail-lights vanish slowly into the blocks of surrounding buildings, maybe a quarter of a mile from the middle of the desolation.

And what is it that lies between these purposeless streets? There is not a whole brick, a foundation to stumble across, a drainpipe, a smashed fowlhouse; the entire place has been razed flat, dug over, and smoothed down again. The bald curve of the hillside shows quite clearly here, near its crown, where the brilliant road, stacked close on either side with warehouses and shops, runs out towards the west. Down below, the district that fills the hollow is impenetrably black. The streets there are so close and so twisted among their massive tenements that it is impossible to trace the line of a single one of them by its lights. The lamps that can be seen shine oddly, and at mysterious distances, as if they were in a marsh. Only the great flat-roofed factory shows clear by its bulk, stretching across three or four whole blocks just below the edge of the waste, with solid rows of lit windows.

Lullaby and Exhortation for the Unwilling Hero

A fish,
Firelight,
A watery ceiling:
Under the door
The drunk wind sleeps.

The bell in the river,
The loaf half eaten,
The coat of the sky.

A pear,
Perfume,
A white glade of curtains:
Out in the moonlight
The smoke reaches high.

The statue in the cellar,
The skirt on the chairback,
The throat of the street.

A shell,
Shadow,
A floor spread with silence:
Faint on the skylight
The fat moths beat.

The pearl in the stocking,
The coals left to die,
The bell in the river,

The loaf half eaten,
The coat of the sky.

The night slides like a thaw
And oil drums bang together.

A frosted-glass door opening, then another.
Orange and blue *décor.*
The smoke that hugs the ceiling tastes of pepper.

What steps descend, what rails conduct?
Sodium bulbs equivocate,
And cowls of ventilators
With limewashed breath hint at the places
To which the void lift cages plunge or soar.

Prints on the landing walls
Are all gone blind with steam;
A voice under the floor
Swings a dull axe against a door.

The gaping office block of night
Shudders into the deep sky overhead:

Thrust down your foot in sleep
Among its depths. Do not respect
The janitors in bed,
The balustrades of iron bars,
The gusty stairwells; thrust it deep,
Into a concrete garage out of sight,
And rest among the cars
That, shut in filtered moonlight,
Sweat mercury and lead.

Subway trains, or winds of indigo,
Bang oil-drums in the yard for war:
Already, half-built towers
Over the bombed city
Show mouths that soon will speak no more,
Stoppered with the perfections of tomorrow.

You can lie women in your bed
With glass and mortar in their hair.
Pocket the key, and draw the curtains,
They'll not care.

Letters on a sweetshop window:
At last the rain slides them askew,
The foetus in the dustbin moves one claw.

And from the locomotive
That's halted on the viaduct
A last white rag of steam
Blows ghostly across the gardens.
When you wake, what will you do?

Under the floorboards of your dream
Gun barrels rolled in lint
Jockey the rooms this way and that.
Across the suburbs, squares of colour gleam:
Swaddled in pink and apricot,
The people are 'making love'.

Those are bright points that flicker
Softly, and vanish one by one.
Your telegraphic fingers mutter the world.
What will they reach for when your sleep is done?

The hiss of tyres along the gutter,
Odours of polish in the air;
A car sleeps in the neighbouring room,
A wardrobe by its radiator.

The rumbling canisters beat for you
Who are a room now altogether bare,
An open mouth pressed outwards against life,
Tasting the sleepers' breath,
The palms of hands, discarded shoes,
Lilac wood, the blade of a breadknife.

Before dawn in the sidings,
Over whose even tracks
Fat cooling towers caress the sky,
The rows of trucks
Extend: black, white,
White, grey, white, black,
Black, white, black, grey,
Marshalled like building blocks:

Women are never far away.

In the century that has passed since this city has become great, it has twice laid itself out in the shape of a wheel. The ghost of the older one still lies among the spokes of the new, those dozen highways that thread constricted ways through the inner suburbs, then thrust out, twice as wide, across the housing estates and into the countryside, dragging moraines of buildings with them. Sixty or seventy years ago there were other main roads, quite as important as these were then, but lying between their paths. By day they are simply alternatives, short cuts, lined solidly with parked cars and crammed with delivery vans. They look merely like side-streets, heartlessly overblown in some excess of Victorian expansion. By night, or on a Sunday, you can see them for what they are. They are still lit meagrely, and the long rows of houses, three and four storeys high, rear black above the lamps enclosing the roadways, clamping them off from whatever surrounds them. From these pavements you can sometimes see the sky at night, not obscured as it is in most parts of the city by the greenish-blue haze of light that steams out of the mercury vapour lamps. These streets are not worth lighting. The houses have not been turned into shops – they are not villas either that might have become offices, but simply tall dwellings, opening straight off the street, with cavernous entries leading into back courts.

The people who live in them are mostly very old. Some have lived through three wars, some through only one; wars of newspapers, of mysterious sciences, of coercion, of disappearance. Wars that have come down the streets from the unknown city and the unknown world, like rainwater floods in the gutters. There are small shops at street corners, with blank rows of houses between them; and taverns carved only shallowly into the massive walls. When these people go into the town, the buses they travel in stop just before they reach it, in the sombre back streets behind the Town Hall and the great insurance offices.

These lost streets are decaying only very slowly. The impacted lives of their inhabitants, the meaninglessness of news, the dead black of the chimney breasts, the conviction that the wind itself comes only from the next street, all wedge together to keep destruction out, to deflect the eye of the developer. And when destruction comes, it is total: the printed notices on the walls, block by block, a few doors left open at night, broken windows advancing down a street until fallen slates appear on the pavement and are not kicked away. Then, after a few weeks of this, the machines arrive.

The Entertainment of War

I saw the garden where my aunt had died
And her two children and a woman from next door;
It was like a burst pod filled with clay.

A mile away in the night I had heard the bombs
Sing and then burst themselves between cramped houses
With bright soft flashes and sounds like banging doors;

The last of them crushed the four bodies into the ground,
Scattered the shelter, and blasted my uncle's corpse
Over the housetop and into the street beyond.

Now the garden lay stripped and stale; the iron shelter
Spread out its separate petals around a smooth clay saucer,
Small, and so tidy it seemed nobody had ever been there.

When I saw it, the house was blown clean by blast and care:
Relations had already torn out the new fireplaces;
My cousin's pencils lasted me several years.

And in his office notepad that was given me
I found solemn drawings in crayon of blondes without dresses.
In his lifetime I had not known him well.

These were the things I noticed at ten years of age;
Those, and the four hearses outside our house,
The chocolate cakes, and my classmates' half-shocked envy.

But my grandfather went home from the mortuary
And for five years tried to share the noises in his skull,
Then he walked out and lay under a furze-bush to die.

When my father came back from identifying the daughter
He asked us to remind him of her mouth.
We tried. He said 'I think it was the one'.

These were marginal people I had met only rarely
And the end of the whole household meant that no grief was seen;
Never have people seemed so absent from their own deaths.

This bloody episode of four whom I could understand better dead
Gave me something I needed to keep a long story moving;
I had no pain of it; can find no scar even now.

But had my belief in the fiction not been thus buoyed up
I might, in the sigh and strike of the next night's bombs
Have realised a little what they meant, and for the first time been afraid.

North Area

Those whom I love avoid all mention of it,
Though certain gestures they've in common
Persuade me they know it well:
A place where I can never go.

No point in asking why, or why not.
I picture it, though –
There must be dunes with cement walks,
A twilight of aluminium
Among beach huts and weather-stained handrails;
Much glass to reflect the clouds;
And a glint of blood in the cat-ice that holds the rushes.

The edge of the city. A low hill with houses on one side
and rough common land on the other, stretching down to
where a dye-works lies along the valley road. Pithead gears
thrust out above the hawthorn bushes; everywhere prefab-
ricated workshops jut into the fields and the allotments.
The society of singing birds and the society of mechanical
hammers inhabit the world together, slightly ruffled and
confined by each other's presence.

By the Pond

This is bitter enough: the pallid water
With yellow rushes crowding toward the shore,
That fishermen's shack,

The pit-mound's taut and staring wire fences,
The ashen sky. All these can serve as conscience.
For the rest, I'll live.

Brick-dust in sunlight. That is what I see now in the city,
a dry epic flavour, whose air is human breath. A place of
walls made straight with plumbline and trowel, to desiccate
and crumble in the sun and smoke. Blistered paint on
cisterns and girders, cracking to show the priming. Old
men spit on the paving slabs, little boys urinate; and the
sun dries it as it dries out patches of damp on plaster
facings to leave misshapen stains. I look for things here
that make old men and dead men seem young. Things
which have escaped, the landscapes of many childhoods.

Wharves, the oldest parts of factories, tarred gable ends
rearing to take the sun over lower roofs. Soot, sunlight,
brick-dust; and the breath that tastes of them.

At the time when the great streets were thrust out along
the old highroads and trackways, the houses shouldering
towards the country and the back streets filling in the

240

widening spaces between them like webbed membranes, the power of will in the town was more open, less speciously democratic, than it is now. There were, of course, cottage railway stations, a jail that pretended to be a castle out of Grimm, public urinals surrounded by screens of cast-iron lacework painted green and scarlet; but there was also an arrogant ponderous architecture that dwarfed and terrified the people by its sheer size and functional brutality: the workhouses and the older hospitals, the thick-walled abattoir, the long vaulted market-halls, the striding canal bridges and railway viaducts. Brunel was welcome here. Compared with these structures the straight white blocks and concrete roadways of today are a fairground, a clear dream just before waking, the creation of salesmen rather than of engineers. The new city is bred out of a hard will, but as it appears, it shows itself a little ingratiating, a place of arcades, passages, easy ascents, good light. The eyes twinkle, beseech and veil themselves; the full, hard mouth, the broad jaw – these are no longer made visible to all.

A street half a mile long with no buildings, only a continuous embankment of sickly grass along one side, with railway signals on it, and strings of trucks through whose black-spoked wheels you can see the sky; and for the whole length of the other a curving wall of bluish brick, caked with soot and thirty feet high. In it, a few wicket gates painted ochre, and fingermarked, but never open. Cobbles in the roadway.

A hundred years ago this was almost the edge of town. The goods yards, the gasworks and the coal stores were established on tips and hillocks in the sparse fields that lay among the houses. Between this place and the centre, a mile or two up the hill, lay a continuous huddle of low streets and courts, filling the marshy valley of the meagre river that now flows under brick and tarmac. And this was as far as the railway came, at first. A great station was built, towering and stony. The sky above it was southerly. The stately approach, the long curves of wall, still remain, but the place is a goods depot with most of its doors barred and pots of geraniums at those windows that are not shuttered. You come upon it suddenly in its open prospect out of tangled streets of small factories. It draws light to itself, especially at sunset, standing still and smooth faced, looking westwards at the hill. I am not able to imagine the activity that must once have been here. I can see no ghosts of men and women, only the gigantic ghost of stone. They are too frightened of it to pull it down.

The Sun Hacks

The sun hacks at the slaughterhouse campanile,
And by the butchers' cars, packed tail-to-kerb,
Masks under white caps wake into human faces.

The river shudders as dawn drums on its culvert;
On the first bus nightworkers sleep, or stare
At hoardings that look out on yesterday.

242

The whale-back hill assumes its concrete city:
The white-flanked towers, the stillborn monuments;
The thousand golden offices, untenanted.

At night on the station platform, near a pile of baskets, a
couple embraced, pressed close together and swaying a
little. It was hard to see where the girl's feet and legs
were. The suspicion this aroused soon caused her hands,
apparently joined behind her lover's back, to become a
small brown paper parcel under the arm of a stout
engine-driver who leaned, probably drunk, against the
baskets, his cap so far forward as almost to conceal his
face. I could not banish the thought that what I had first
seen was in fact his own androgynous fantasy, the self-
sufficient core of his stupor. Such a romantic thing, so
tender, for him to contain. He looked more comic and
complaisant than the couple had done, and more likely to
fall heavily to the floor.

A café with a frosted glass door through which much light
is diffused. A tall young girl comes out and stands in front
of it, her face and figure quite obscured by this milky
radiance.

She treads out on to a lopsided ochre panel of lit pavement
before the doorway and becomes visible as a coloured shape,
moving sharply. A wrap of honey and ginger, a flared saffron
skirt, grey-white shoes. She goes off past the Masonic
Temple with a young man: he is pale, with dark hair and
a shrunken, earnest face. You could imagine him a size

larger. Just for a moment, as it happens, there is no one else in the street at all. Their significance escapes rapidly like a scent, before the footsteps vanish among the car engines.

A man in the police court. He looked dapper and poker-faced, his arms straight, the long fingers just touching the hem of his checked jacket. Four days after being released from the prison where he had served two years for theft he had been discovered at midnight clinging like a tree-shrew to the bars of a glass factory-roof. He made no attempt to explain his presence there; the luminous nerves that made him fly up to it were not visible in daylight, and the police seemed hardly able to believe this was the creature they had brought down in the darkness.

In this city the governing authority is limited and mean: so limited that it can do no more than preserve a superficial order. It supplies fuel, water and power. It removes a fair proportion of the refuse, cleans the streets after a fashion, and discourages fighting. With these things, and a few more of the same sort, it is content. This could never be a capital city for all its size. There is no mind in it, no regard. The sensitive, the tasteful, the fashionable, the intolerant and powerful, have not moved through it as they have moved through London, evaluating it, altering it deliberately, setting in motion wars of feeling about it. Most of it has never been seen.

In an afternoon of dazzling sunlight in the thronged streets,
I saw at first no individuals but a composite monster, its
unfeeling surfaces matted with dust: a mass of necks, limbs
without extremities, trunks without heads; unformed stirrings
and shovings spilling across the streets it had managed to
get itself provided with.

Later, as the air cooled, flowing loosely about the buildings
that stood starkly among the declining rays, the creature
began to divide and multiply. At crossings I could see
people made of straws, rags, cartons, the stuffing of burst
cushions, kitchen refuse. Outside the Grand Hotel, a long-
boned carrot-haired girl with glasses, loping along, and
with strips of bright colour, rich, silky green and blue, in
her soft clothes. For a person made of such scraps she
was beautiful.

Faint blue light dropping down through the sparse leaves
of the plane trees in the churchyard opposite after sundown,
cooling and shaping heads, awakening eyes.

The Hill behind the Town

Sullen hot noon, a loop of wire,
With zinc light standing everywhere,
A glint on the chapels,
Glint on the chapels.

Under my heel a loop of wire
Dragged in the dust is earth's wide eye,
Unseen for days,
Unseen days.

Geranium-wattled, fenced in wire,
Caged white cockerels crowd near
And stretch red throats,
Stretch red throats;

Their cries tear grievous through taut wire,
Drowned in tanks of factory sirens
At sullen noon,
Sullen hot noon.

The day's on end; a loop of wire
Kicked from the dust's bleak daylight leaves
A blind white world,
Blind white world.

The Poplars

Where the road divides
Just out of town
By the wall beyond the filling-station
Four Lombardy poplars
Brush stiff against the moorland wind.

Clarity is in their tops
That no one can touch
Till they are felled,
Brushwood to cart away:

To know these tall pointers
I need to withdraw
From what is called my life
And from my net
Of achievable desires.

Why should their rude and permanent virginity
So capture me? Why should studying
These lacunae of possibility
Relax the iron templates of obligation
Leaving me simply Man?

All I have done, or can do
Is prisoned in its act:
I think I am afraid of becoming
A cemetery of performance.

Starting to Make a Tree

First we carried out the faggot of steel stakes; they varied
in length, though most were taller than a man.

We slid one free of the bundle and drove it into the
ground, first padding the top with rag, that the branch
might not be injured with leaning on it.

Then we took turns to choose stakes of the length we wanted, and to feel for the distances between them. We gathered to thrust them firmly in.

There were twenty or thirty of them in all; and when they were in place we had, round the clearing we had left for the trunk, an irregular radial plantation of these props, each with its wad of white at the tip. It was to be an old, down-curving tree.

This was in keeping with the burnt, chemical blue of the soil, and the even hue of the sky which seemed to have been washed with a pale brownish smoke;

another clue was the flatness of the horizon on all sides except the north, where it was broken by the low slate or tarred shingle roofs of the houses, which stretched away from us for a mile or more.

This was the work of the morning. It was done with care, for we had no wish to make revisions;

we were, nonetheless, a little excited, and hindered the women at their cooking in our anxiety to know whose armpit and whose groin would help us most in the modelling of the bole, and the thrust of the boughs.

That done, we spent the early dusk of the afternoon gathering materials from the nearest houses; and there was plenty:

a great flock mattress; two carved chairs; cement; chicken-wire; tarpaulin; a smashed barrel; lead piping; leather of all kinds; and many small things.

In the evening we sat late, and discussed how we could best use them. Our tree was to be very beautiful.

Yet whenever I see that some of these people around me are bodily in love, I feel it is my own energy, my own hope, tension and sense of time in hand, that have gathered and vanished down that dark drain; it is I who am left, shivering and exhausted, to try and kick the lid back into place so that I can go on without the fear of being able to feel only vertically, like a blind wall, or thickly, like the tyres of a bus.

Lovers turn to me faces of innocence where I would expect wariness. They have disappeared for entire hours into the lit holes of life, instead of lying stunned on its surface as I, and so many, do for so long; or instead of raising their heads cautiously and scenting the manifold airs that blow through the streets.

The city asleep. In it there are shadows that are sulphurous, tanks of black bile. The glitter on the roadways is the deceptive ore that shines on coal.

The last buses have left the centre; the pallid faces of the crowd looked like pods, filled by a gusty summer that had come too late for plenty.

Silvered rails that guide pedestrians at street corners stand useless. Towards midnight, or at whatever hour the sky descends with its full iron weight, the ceilings drop lower everywhere; each light is partial, and proper only to its place. There is no longer any general light, only particular lights that overlap.

Out of the swarming thoroughfares, the night makes its own streets with a rake that drags persuaded people out of its way: streets where the bigger buildings have already swung themselves round to odd angles against the weakened currents of the traffic.

There are lamplit streets where the full darkness is only in the deep drains and in the closed eyesockets and shut throats of the old as they lie asleep; their breath moves red tunnel-lights.

The main roads hold their white-green lights with difficulty, like long, loaded boughs; when the machines stop moving down them their gradients reappear.

Journeys at night: sometimes grooves in a thick substance, sometimes raised weals on black skin.

The city at night has no eye, any more than it has by day, although you would expect to find one; and over much of it the sleep is aqueous and incomplete, like that of a hospital ward.

But to some extent it stops, drops and congeals. It could be broken like asphalt, and the men and women rolled out like sleeping maggots.

Once I wanted to prove the world was sick. Now I want to prove it healthy. The detection of sickness means that death has established itself as an element of the timetable; it has come within the range of the measurable. Where there is no time there is no sickness.

The Wind at Night

The suburb lies like a hand tonight,
A man's thick hand, so stubborn
No child or poet can move it.

The wind drives itself mad with messages,
Clattering train wheels over the roofs,
Collapsing streets of sound until
Far towers, daubed with swollen light,
Lunge closer to abuse it,

This suburb like a sleeping hand,
With helpless elms that shudder
Angry between its fingers,
Powerless to disprove it.

And, although the wind derides
The spaces of this stupid quarter,
And sets the time of night on edge,
It mocks the hand, but cannot lose it:

This stillness keeps us in the flesh,
For us to use it.

I stare into the dark; and I see a window, a large sash window of four panes, such as might be found in the living-room of any fair-sized old house. Its curtains are drawn back and it looks out on to a small damp garden, narrow close at hand where the kitchen and outhouses lead back, and then almost square. Privet and box surround it, and the flowerbeds are empty save for a few laurels or rhododendrons, some leafless rose shrubs and a giant yucca. It is a December afternoon, and it is raining. Not far from the window is a black marble statue of a long-haired, long-bearded old man. His robes are conventionally archaic, and he sits, easily enough, on what seems a pile of small boulders, staring intently and with a look of great intelligence towards the patch of wall just under the kitchen window. The statue looks grimy, but its exposed surfaces are highly polished by the rain, so that the nose and the cheekbones stand out strongly in the gloom. It is rather smaller than life-size. It is clearly not in its proper place: resting as it does across the moss of the raised border, it is appreciably tilted forward and to one side, almost as if it had been abandoned as too heavy by those who were trying to move it – either in or out.

Walking through the suburb at night, as I pass the dentist's house I hear a clock chime a quarter, a desolate brassy sound. I know where it stands, on the mantelpiece in the still surgery. The chime falls back into the house, and beyond it, without end. Peace.

I sense the simple nakedness of these tiers of sleeping men and women beneath whose windows I pass. I imagine it in its own setting, a mean bathroom in a house no longer new, a bathroom with plank panelling, painted a peculiar shade of green by an amateur, and badly preserved. It is full of steam, so much as to obscure the yellow light and hide the high, patched ceiling. In this dream, standing quiet, the private image of the householder or his wife, damp and clean.

I see this as it might be floating in the dark, as if the twinkling point of a distant street-lamp had blown in closer, swelling and softening to a foggy oval. I can call up a series of such glimpses that need have no end, for they are all the bodies of strangers. Some are deformed or diseased, some are ashamed, but the peace of humility and weakness is there in them all.

I have often felt myself to be vicious, in living so much by the eye, yet among so many people. I can be afraid that the egg of light through which I see these bodies might present itself as a keyhole. Yet I can find no sadism in the way I see them now. They are warm-fleshed, yet their shapes have the minuscule, remote morality of some mediaeval woodcut of the Expulsion: an eternally startled Adam, a permanently bemused Eve. I see them as homunculi, moving privately each in a softly lit fruit in a nocturnal tree. I can consider without scorn or envy the well-found bedrooms I pass, walnut and rose-pink, altars of tidy, dark-haired women, bare-backed, wifely. Even in these I can see order.

I come quite often now upon a sort of ecstasy, a rag of light blowing among the things I know, making me feel I am not the one for whom it was intended, that I have inadvertently been looking through another's eyes and have seen what I cannot receive.

I want to believe I live in a single world. That is why I am keeping my eyes at home while I can. The light keeps on separating the world like a table knife: it sweeps across what I see and suggests what I do not. The imaginary comes to me with as much force as the real, the remembered with as much force as the immediate. The countries on the map divide and pile up like ice-floes: what is strange is that I feel no stress, no grating discomfort among the confusion, no loss; only a belief that I should not be here. I see the iron fences and the shallow ditches of the countryside the mild wind has travelled over. I cannot enter that countryside; nor can I escape it. I cannot join together the mild wind and the shallow ditches, I cannot lay the light across the world and then watch it slide away. Each thought is at once translucent and icily capricious. A polytheism without gods.

The Park

If you should go there on such a day –
The red sun disappearing,
Netted behind black sycamores;

If you should go there on such a day –
The sky drawn thin with frost,
Its cloud-rims bright and bitter –

If you should go there on such a day,
Maybe the old goose will chase you away.

If you should go there to see
The shallow concrete lake,
Scummed over, fouled with paper;

If you should go there to see
The grass plots, featureless,
Muddy, and bruised, and balding –

If you should go there to see,
Maybe the old goose will scare you as he scared me

Waddling fast on his diseased feet,
His orange bill thrust out,
His eyes indignant;

Waddling fast on his diseased feet,
His once-ornamental feathers
Baggy, and smeared with winter –

Waddling fast on his diseased feet,
The old goose will one day reach death; and be unfit to eat.

And when the goose is dead, then we
Can say we're able, at last,
No longer hindered from going;

And when the goose is dead, then we
Have the chance, if we still want it,
To wander the park at leisure;

– Oh, when excuse is dead, then we
Must visit there, most diligently.

Notes

Excerpts from *Roy Fisher: A Bibliography* by Derek Slade

City, Worcester, Migrant Press; date of publication given as May 1961, actually appeared June 1961. An edition of approximately 300 copies. This version of *City* contains prose paragraphs and three poems – 'The Judgment', 'Do Not Remain Too Much Alone' and 'Toyland' – omitted from the revised *City* printed in the Fulcrum Press *Collected Poems 1968*. Neither 'The Judgment' nor 'Do Not Remain Too Much Alone' has been printed elsewhere. 'Toyland' appeared as a separate poem in *Collected Poems 1968*, *Poems 1955-1980*, *Poems 1955-1987*, *The Dow Low Drop* and both editions of *The Long and the Short of It*.

Then Hallucinations, Worcester, Migrant Press, 1962. An edition of approximately 200 copies.

'Toyland' (10 February 1957)

City (Migrant Press edition only)

Combustion, 4

Children of Albion

Looking Glass

Widening Circles: Five Black Country Poets, ed. Edward Lowbury. Stafford, West Midland Arts, 1976.

Englische Lyrik der Gegenwart: Gedichte ab 1945, ed. Michael Butler and Ilsabe Arnold-Dielewicz. Munich, C.H. Beck, 1981 (English text and translation into German by the editors).

Contemporary British Poetry: Patterns from the 1950s to the Present Day

The Hutchinson Book of Post-War British Poetry, ed. Dannie Abse. London, Hutchinson, 1989.

The Harvill Book of Twentieth Century Poetry in English, ed. Michael Schmidt. London, Harvill Press, 1999.

New Penguin Book of English Verse, ed. Paul Keegan. London, Penguin Books, 2000

Collected: *CP68, P55–80, P55–87, DLD, LSI, LSI2*

'Night Walkers' (3 August 1960)

Living Arts, 1, 1963, ed. Theo Crosby and John Bodley (as part of *City*, though this poem was not included either in the Migrant *City* or the subsequent revised version).

Collected: *S*

'The Judgment' (24 August 1960)

Collected: *City* (Migrant edition only)

City

Prose sections mainly 1959

'Lullaby and Exhortation for the Unwilling Hero' (3–13 August 1960)

Britische Lyrik der Gegenwart: Eine Zwei Sprachige Anthologie, ed. Iain Galbraith. Mainz, Joachim Hempel, 1984. English text and translation into German by Martha Peach.

'The Entertainment of War' (23 January 1957)

Ikon, 1:4, March 1966

Children of Albion

Echinox, 1973, Romania, Clug (translated into Romanian by Dimitri Coicoi-Pop).

The Faber Book of Modern Verse (4th ed.), ed. Michael Roberts, rev. Peter Porter. London, Faber & Faber, 1982.

The Penguin Book of Poetry from Britain and Ireland since 1945, ed. Simon Armitage and Robert Crawford. London, Penguin, 1998.

Not to Speak of the Dog: 101 Short Stories in Verse, ed. Christopher Reid, London, Faber & Faber, 2000.

Anthology of Twentieth-Century British and Irish Poetry, ed. Keith Tuma, New York, Oxford University Press, 2001.

The Hundred Years' War: modern war poems, ed. Neil Astley. Hexham, Bloodaxe Books, 2014.

'North Area' (19 August 1960)
Widening Circles

'By the Pond' (2 June 1957)
The Firebox: Poetry from Britain and Ireland after 1945, ed. Sean O'Brien. London, Picador, 1998.
New Penguin Book of English Verse

'The Sun Hacks' (1 September 1960)
Extra Verse, 8 (entitled 'The Valley Hacks')
Steaua, 1973, Romania, Clug (translated into Romanian by Dimitri Coicoi-Pop).
Poems of Warwickshire

'The Hill Behind the Town' (8 June 1959)

'The Poplars' (5 February 1957)
Combustion, 4

Migrant, 5

Anthology of Twentieth-Century British and Irish Poetry

'Starting to Make a Tree' (28 December 1960)

Jazz Poems, ed. Anselm Hollo. Vista Books, 1963.

Poetmeat, 8, n.d. (c. 1965), ed. Dave Cunliffe and Tina Morris, Blackburn, Lancs.

Poetmeat, 13, Spring 1967, ed. Dave Cunliffe and Tina Morris, Blackburn, Lancs.

Children of Albion

Steaua, 1973 (translated into Romanian by Dimitri Coicoi-Pop).

Giovani Poeti Inglesi (English text and translation into Italian by Renato Oliva)

The Orchard Book of Poems, ed. Adrian Mitchell. London, Orchard Books, 1993.

Red Sky at Night: An Anthology of British Socialist Poetry, ed. Andy Croft and Adrian Mitchell, Nottingham, Five Leaves Publications, 2003

'The Wind at Night' (10 January 1961)

Outposts, 49, Summer 1961, ed. Howard Sergeant, Dulwich Village.

Jazz Poems

Alembic, 4, Winter 1975-76, ed. Robert Hampson, London.

Widening Circles

Windows, 2 February 1977.

'The Park' (21 February 1961)

Widening Circles

Prose-section beginning 'Walking through the suburb...'

    Anthology of Twentieth-Century British and Irish Poetry

    Here to Eternity: An Anthology of Poetry, ed. Andrew Motion, London, Faber & Faber, 2001.

    City was printed in its entirety in *Living Arts* 1, with the variations noted above, and in *Twenty-Three Modern British Poets*, ed. John Matthias. Chicago, Swallow Press, 1971.

    Collected: *CP68, P55-80, P55-87, DLD, LSI, LSI2. SP* contains three prose sections from *City*, plus 'The Entertainment of War', 'The Sun Hacks', 'The Poplars' and 'Starting to Make a Tree'.

Roy Fisher's published comments on *City*

1.

Most of the 'City' writing is meant to be about a city which has already turned into a city of the mind. Where the writing is topographical it's meant to do with the EFFECTS of topography, the creation of scenic moments, psychological environments, and it's not meant to be an historical/spatial city entailed to empirical reality.

2.

When I was writing the 'City' poems, and particularly this is when I was first writing with any sort of sense of something that I must do for myself (and this was around the time of late 20s, time of being 30); when I was doing that I quite simply had a sense of place which was not culturally extensive, it didn't extend into history at all, even though in the 'City' pieces I invoke the 19th-century culture versus the 20th century culture. But historically that's very simple, it's really of little subtlety, and it doesn't, as it were, attempt to invoke the historical meaning of the behaviour of the people on the ground in anything like the way Olson does.

What I was faced with was something quite personal, which was the sensation of having lived for a very long time (and I'm not a traveller at all, I stay very much in one place), having lived for a very long time in and having had my consciousness of, a particular large and nondescript undesigned environment which was, as it happened, an expanding industrial city, which was a deposit of all sorts of inadvertent by-products of ideas. In many cases the cultural ideas, the economic ideas, had disappeared into the graveyards of people who had the ideas. But the by-products in things like street layouts, domestic architecture, where the schools were, how anything happened – all these things were left all over the place as a sort of script, an indecipherable script with no key. And the interesting thing for me was that the culture, particularly the metropolitan culture, the literary culture, had no alphabet to offer for simply talking about what I saw all the time. I mean, when I say in 'City', 'most of it's never been seen', it's a provocative phrase: it wasn't verbalised, it wasn't talked about. And there I wasn't interested really at all in the particular city, but in the phenomenon of having a perceptual environment which was taken as read, which was taken as to be assumed and not a thing for which any vocabulary needed to exist. Consequently in historical terms that need only to be very thin. I was talking about really my own time. And in the work I'd be bouncing the feelings I had, which were the feelings of a rather belated adolescence. I was coming back to the city in my late twenties at a time when it was being rebuilt. And I was also in a state of life when I could remember childhood – I was far enough away from childhood to have an intensity about some memories. And again I'd had a fairly inarticulate childhood, a childhood where I had a lot of sensations going in, but not a very – you know, I wasn't a child writer or anything of that sort, a child reader. There were still things left in my own perception which were unsorted. And there was another thing which was again merely personal – my father was dying, and he was very closely associated with the city, with these areas over a period of forty years. Seeing this life ending, and the inevitable process of turning up old photographs, old apprenticeship papers, extended time that made you realise more than usually how much the place was dependent upon very evanescent, temporal, subjective renderings, which might never BE rendered. And at that point my own lifetime was extended through his.

3.

You have to distinguish between 'City' and the other things. *The Ship's Orchestra* and *The Cut Pages* are composed works, they stand as they were composed, and if you'd have seen them before they were finished you would have found them as they are (except the closing pages, which were unwritten), unaltered, and they were composed as they stand. 'City' and some of the other prose pieces in *Cut Pages* – those are assemblages, they're albums. And 'City' is carved from half a dozen notebooks, poems written in various towns or about various towns or no town at all. In fact it was Michael Shayer's idea that the sort of perceptual attentions given to urban things could make a work on its own. I'd been, part of the time, writing a rather pretentious pseudo-novel. I admit I was interested in the idea of a prose diary, and kept things like that. I was interested in Rilke's writing about Paris, Kafka's journals, Cocteau's things like *Opium*, and so I got the makings of it there. But the idea of that particular thing was not compositional it was editorial.

4.

Mike Shayer. *He* done it! The thing about that was that I had written – I'll tell you this story if you are going to keep the tape, because otherwise it might get forgotten. People who have read my stuff tend largely to have read 'City', particularly if they are not specialists in poetry. The odd pieces that are in an anthology, the things that get discussed in a seminar, tend to be pieces of the 'City' stuff. But what happened with that writing was that I felt free to talk about physical things, the actual surroundings of the city I was born in. I felt particularly free since nobody was printing my stuff, this was rather good, I felt that there was a work there. At this time I was about 29 or 30, and had no sense of cleaning up my writing at all really; it was still very callow and very unlicked and indulgent. And the interesting thing was this: I was keeping notebooks, noticing all kinds of things, and writing odd spin-off pieces of verse, and I realised that there must be something there and I started to write a work called 'The Citizen' which was – well, 'City' now seems to me to be over-written, and the last time it was published I went through it removing adjectives. I think you, in your article [*Stand*, vol. 11, no. 1, 1969-70], still found a few I could have removed further, and indeed, I could cut it and cut it and cut it down to, if it has got any bones … I could carry on quite a long way; but I was still taking adjectives out of it a few years ago. But the work from which it was cut, was, in fact, a much more floriferous and squashy thing; it was called 'The Citizen', and it was a very aspiring and oddly self-romanticising work. It had German romanticism, it had Lawrence Durrell, all kinds of things, and it didn't have anything I would have called a stiff confidence in it; but I wrote it, and ran it into the ground. It was a long manuscript by my standards, twenty or thirty thousand words. It was getting on for a short novel which had everything in it. Then I sort of broke it up and left it lying about; and Michael Shayer, who had both studied with Leavis and done a lot of Black Mountain homework, saw that there was an interesting assemblage to be made, and together we made assemblages. (We were starting to do little pamphlets.) I made an assemblage which would satisfy me, and it was an extremely symmetrical assemblage; it was very safe and trim and well organised by the standards I had then; Michael, who was being a very hard man at that point said: no, it is all sewn up; and I said, '*You* try' – in more or less those terms. He got the scissors out and cut my manuscript around, jiggled it again, and as far as I could see, there was not a self that I could present in it; they were just my bits; so I let it go. The first version was that, and I found it extremely uncomfortable to live with. I reorganised this into a tidier version, but I don't know how far I was interested in retidying it at all. I think he was, as it were, arranging it into a drama that wasn't in my original plan at all. He was taking it over the lines that I was writing within. [...] he plotted it more than I did. Now, he plotted it in a disjointed and raw and somewhat schizoid fashion; I had plotted it in a romantic, resolutionary, pessimistic fashion, some of which I restored to it in the editing. There is a sort of rather well-written yearning towards the end which is satisfying in a way but which I'd regard as rather too much on a plate now. But that is in the background of it all; the original assemblage wasn't mine. I had given up.

5.

If I look in myself for anything that might be called nostalgia for things gone, what I find is anything but the usual parade of well-loved, fondly remembered public focal points, particular pubs, theatres, cafes and customs, that could add up to a vanished way of social life. When I was a student and a denizen of the city centre I lived on a circuit of places of that kind – Mason College, Yates's Wine Lodge, the Mecca Casino, the Reference Library, the Troc., the Kardomah, and an extraordinary café called Nick's, which had an atmosphere like the bottom of a drain – but only for a while. My real recollections are of private and aimless impressions, glimpses down strange streets, blistering sunlight on giant bridge girders, the smell of coalyards – idylls and hells made out of the only materials to hand. Most of all I remember the conviction that always, just over the next built-up skylight but one, there were unseen worlds, romantic because unseen but inevitably made of just the same constituents as the small patch I knew.

These were not evaluations that passed with childhood. They lasted through adolescence and a few years of absence, and were still accessible when I returned to Birmingham in the late 1950s. The reconstructions were just then starting, late and slow. Demolitions and excavations looked casual and piecemeal though on an epic scale. For a while they seemed to express and add to the older city, while in reality they were signalling its end. All the options still seemed open. In those days I was living in the city on an odd life-rhythm. As a part-time jazz-club musician I was often going to work just as everybody else went home; I would be hanging about at times when others were purposeful; I would be crossing town after midnight; if I slept badly I would be taking aimless bus journeys at six in the morning and walking remote suburbs where I knew nobody. All this intensified my habit of looking obliquely at things, thinking thoughts about them which were no part of the original design, and it generated the prose-and-poetry sequence 'City', which is essentially of that period. Earlier, the impressions would have had no urgency; later they could not have existed.

6.

It's something to do with the fact that the sort of sensibility I had in the 'City' period, through the block which followed and, at a fair remove to the late sixties – it was a very phobic personality. 'City', for instance, is very much bits that are left from a very hairy epic novel-cum-poem. And if you look at the self-structures or the narratives – the buried narrative – or the quasi-dramatic situations in the older work there is nearly always a myth of a person who leaves life.

7.

But certainly there was a grim period – the *City* period – where the noise I wanted to make was an extra injection of blackness, an extra darkness of the aesthetic, so that I actually wanted to make menacing works in my isolation, if you like.

8.

There's a change from the 'City' work in that I very carefully didn't use a named Birmingham at that point, partly because I was doing something a bit like the work of a novelist who just gives himself the ordinary licence of changing Oxford, Mississippi, into Jefferson or Dorchester into Casterbridge, the ordinary license of avoiding the entailments of documentary realism, which would be very heavy for me because I've got photographic optical memory. I have to make the city strange in order to be able to move my mind in it at all. Otherwise I would be just left with super-realism, which would drive me screaming mad because I really can remember window-frames and bricks and things.

9.

I knew perfectly well it had been seen by Auden, with whom I have this very remote family connection, and by MacNeice, and it had been seen by Walter Allen. He wrote some novels about Birmingham in which he'd done all these games of calling it 'The City' and so forth in the 1930s. He was born in about 1911 a few miles from where I was born. I read these novels from a local library when I was a student and I was quite excited to realise that anybody who had seen the place could actually write about it.

10.

Paterson is its antecedent in a historical sense to 'City', but not as part of my own experience. I knew of the

existence of *Paterson*, but didn't see it until after the period
– 1957-60 – when I was writing the very heterogenous and
unplanned mass of texts from which the 'City' constituents
were to be taken. Michael Shayer, who conceived the idea
that a live collage might be extracted from the directionless,
stranded mass, and who indeed made the selection and
arrangement of the 1961 version, had read *Paterson*, and
no doubt had it in mind.

11.

So the work is a curious collaborative hybrid. The *effect*
of the prose/poetry assemblage in 'City' is just as you
describe it, and in that respect the comparison with
Williams is apt, as is the comment about the way in
which both *Paterson* and 'City' differ from 'The Waste
Land'. But the fact remains that the poems used in 'City'
were generated in the usual way of single poems, without
any thought of subsequent incorporation in a longer work,
while the prose pieces had come from another direction.
They'd mostly begin as diary observations, private, not
intended for publication, and written with my own *persona*;
I'd then started to assemble them into a work called 'The
Citizen', which had a romantic and shadowy characterised
'I'. This is the ghost-text which lies under 'City'. The 'I'
in it was, it must be said, wholly voyeuristic, alienated,
de-politicised and a-social: and the text petered out at the
point where, after a couple of hundred pages, I decided
I'd better have him have a conversation with another
human being. He couldn't get a single word out. So that
was the end of him.

12.

The movement in your commentary from your response to my impressionistic reportage to the detection of a lack of a historical critique is interesting. The impressionism was deliberate, and if those passages work at all, then it's as impressionist pieces, without further analysis adumbrated. It seemed to me most important to record symptoms accurately, before even starting a diagnosis. But not solely visually or photographically, any more than by way of the sort of social data I might have hunted out and used but didn't; I also wanted to include the dimension of affect, the imaginative compulsions of living in the place, as a complete sensory environment. I put that first.

13.

In the odd quasi-political asides – *the power of will* and so forth – in 'City', I wasn't reaching in towards a critique; I was, in keeping with my programme, staying on the affective surface, of styles of government, aesthetics of persuasion or constraint. And that connects with your response, appropriate I think, to the exaggerated use of language. I was indeed impelled to a certain expressionism of language by what I experienced and the agonised tropes followed naturally enough; and I was, indeed, deliberately fishing, in a prosperous nowhere-city of the Fifties, for the hidden continuation of the hysteria Brecht and Grosz had seen as open and paramount in the early Twenties: I knew there was a streak of it there and I wanted a way of bringing it out. That's the explanation of my choice of that register in preference to something conversational or conventionally post-imagist.

14.

I found that returning to Birmingham after an absence had given me an artist's distance from it. I wanted to write about it, and became immersed in its associative power. My journeys through it in connection with my educational work and my piano playing were in all directions at all hours of the day and night. I saw it from the oddest of angles. Without any particular aim I started on the voluminous series of prose pieces and poems which I was to help Michael Shayer to edit down to the Migrant pamphlet *City* which appeared, as my first collection, in 1961.

15.

If there were such a thing as an objective correlative, the physical body of the Birmingham I write about, which is almost entirely now an archaic city – which when I wrote about it at first, I wrote about without a name, knowing it was a city of the mind – that was a sort of huge image or symbol for a very elaborate stasis of mind. I can't be more explicit than that or I wouldn't have had to write all those obsessive things about bricks and bits of ground, soil and grit and dog-shit and the light on greasy windows and all that sort of thing. It was just that, it was an externalised picture of a very extensive state or temperamental conundrum, a temperamental fix. Even what Jung would call a complex.

It certainly wasn't done as a responsible journalist or sociologist or political writer would tackle it – it's not done from the analysis of data, it's done from the experience of an overwhelming subjective sense of being possessed by the place and what *A Furnace* does is to go some way towards locating the phases of the obsession with that place, in some sort of intellectual education, you might call it, increased state of understanding.

But yes, it made no pretence to be objective or analytic, there's more of an exorcism about it, as if it were a form of visitation, a demon. I didn't like it, but I was possessed by it.

16.

Forty years ago when I was experiencing the materials of 'City', the Birmingham I collected was virtually synchronous. At its extremes it had no more duration than my father's lifetime: in 1959 he was dying there, at 70. And although it was starting to crumble into demolition and renewal there hung over it a sort of Faulknerian stasis – it was easy for me to lay the atmosphere (though not the plot) of *Light in August* across it. It was still very much what it had been when my father was a boy: the old hierarchical industrial buildup had been halted in the moment of rapid modernisation by the war. It was that twenty-year delay that created the post-bellum stasis; which in its turn made a medium in which my quite intense affective fantasy reading of the city as a stage for one character could grow. For me there was in those days no other reading to be had, or suspected.

Sources

Some of the passages in this section have been reprinted in *An Easily Bewildered Child: Occasional Prose 1963-2013*, ed. Peter Robinson (Bristol, Shearsman Books, 2014) and others in *Interviews Through Time and Selected Prose*, ed. Tony Frazer (Kentisbeare, Devon, Shearsman Books, 2000), and in the 2nd revised edition, *Interviews Through Time*, ed. Tony Frazer (Bristol, Shearsman Books, 2013). Where indicated below, these titles have been abbreviated to *EBC*, *ITT1* and *ITT2* respectively.

1: Jed Rasula and Mike Erwin, 'An Interview with Roy Fisher' (dated 19 November 1973), Roy Fisher, *Nineteen Poems and an Interview* (Pensnett, Staffs: Grosseteste Press, June 1975), pp. 12-38, p. 12, *ITT1*, p. 56 and *ITT2*, p. 34.

2: *Ibid*. pp. 18-19, *ITT1* pp. 61-2, *ITT2* pp. 40-1.

3: *Ibid*. p.34, *ITT1* p. 69, *ITT2* p. 48.

4: 'Conversation with Roy Fisher', transcript of a conversation between RF and Eric Mottram (22 January 1973), *Saturday Morning*, no. 1, London (Spring 1976), un-paginated [p. 16].

5: Roy Fisher, 'Brum Born', *Vole* ed. Richard Boston, no. 4 (1977), pp. 38-39, *EBC*, p. 49.

6: Robert Sheppard, *Turning the Prism: An Interview with Roy Fisher* (London: Toads Damp Press, January 1986), p. 6, *ITT1* p. 76, *ITT2* pp. 56-57. This is a reprint, in booklet form, of the interview published in *Gargoyle*, 24 (Washington DC, 1984), pp. 75-96. The interview took place on 7 June 1982.

7: Sheppard, *Turning the Prism*, p. 8.

8: *Ibid*. pp.9-10, *ITT1*, pp. 7-8, *ITT2*, p. 58.

9: *Ibid*. p.11, *ITT1*, p. 79, *ITT2*, p. 59.

10: Paul Lester and Roy Fisher, *A Birmingham Dialogue* (Birmingham: Protean Publications, 1986), p. 21, *EBC*, p. 112. This pamphlet contains 'The Poetry of Roy Fisher', pp. 5-20, an undergraduate dissertation by Paul Lester written in 1974, and 'Reply to Paul Lester by Roy Fisher', pp. 21-9, written in 1985.

11: *Ibid*. p. 22, *EBC*, pp. 112-13.

12: *Ibid*. pp. 22-23, *EBC*, p. 113.

13: *Ibid*. pp.24-25, *EBC*, pp. 114-15.

14: Roy Fisher, 'Antebiography', *Contemporary Authors* (Autobiography Series), no. 10 (Detroit, New York, Fort Lauderdale, London: Gale Research, 1989), pp. 79-100, p. 98, *EBC*, p. 47.

15: Jonathan Roper, 'An Interview with Roy Fisher', *Disclaimer* no. 2 (Keele University: no date, but published early 1990), un-paginated. The interview took place on 27 September 1989.

16: '"Come to Think of It, the Imagination": Roy Fisher in Conversation with John Kerrigan', *News for the Ear: A Homage to Roy Fisher*, ed. Peter Robinson and Robert Sheppard (Exeter, Stride Publications, 2000), p. 96, *ITT2*, p. 117. The interview was conducted via email between 24 September 1998 and 20 February 1999. It is also available at http://jacketmagazine.com/35/iv-fisher-ivb-kerrigan.shtml.

Secondary Bibliography

Denise Levertov, 'An English Event': review of *City*, *Kulchur*, 2:6 (Summer 1962), pp. 3-9.

Gael Turnbull, 'Some Resonances and Speculations on Reading Roy Fisher's *City*', *Kulchur*, 2:7 (Autumn 1962), pp. 23-29, also published in *Gael Turnbull, More Words: Gael Turnbull on Poets and Poetry*, Gael Turnbull, 2012 (see below).

Eric Mottram, 'Roy Fisher's Work'. Stand, 11:1, 1969-70, pp. 9-18. Also, pp.70-71: review by Robin Fulton of *CP68*.

Ronald Hayman, 'The City and the House': review of *CP68*. *Encounter*, 34:2, February 1970, pp. 84-91.

Donald Davie, *Thomas Hardy and British Poetry* (London: Routledge & Kegan Paul, 1973), pp. 152-79. Chapter 7, 'Roy Fisher: An Appreciation'. Detailed commentary on *City* throughout this chapter. This book was reprinted, together with other essays by Donald Davie, in *With the Grain*, ed. Clive Wilmer (Manchester: Carcanet, 1998).

Jenny Fowler, Review of the Amber LP reading of *City* by RF Gramophone, July 1977, p. 88. Available online at: http://www.gramophone.net/Issue/Page/July%20 1977/ 88/770057/.

Peter Robinson, 'Liberties in Context': review of *P55-80*, *Grosseteste Review*, 13, 1980/81, pp. 83-92. See especially pp. 84-87 for commentary on *City*.

Phillip Gardner, 'A *City* of the Mind': review of *P55-80*, *Times Literary Supplement*, 20 March 1981, p. 314.

Peter Barry, 'Language and the City in Roy Fisher's Poetry', *English Studies: A Journal of English Language and Literature*, 67:3, Lise, Netherlands, June 1986, pp. 234-49.

Robert Sheppard, 'De-Anglicizing the Midlands: The European Context of Roy Fisher's *City*', *English: The Journal of the English Association*, 41:169, spring 1992, pp. 49-70.

Neil Corcoran, *English Poetry since 1940* (London and New York: Longman, 1993), pp. 164-79. Chapter 12, 'Varieties of Neo-Modernism'. See especially pp. 170-72 for commentary on *City*.

Ian Gregson, *Contemporary Poetry and Postmodernism: Dialogue and Estrangement* (London: Macmillan, 1996), pp. 170-91. Chapter 10, 'Music of the Generous Eye: The Poetry of Roy Fisher'.

Nikki Santilli, 'The Prose Poem and the City', *Prose Studies*, 20:1, 1997, pp. 77-89.

Sean O'Brien, 'Roy Fisher: A Polytheism with No Gods', *The Deregulated Muse: Essays on Contemporary British & Irish Poetry* (Newcastle upon Tyne: Bloodaxe Books, 1998), pp. 112-22.

Peter Barry, *Contemporary British Poetry and the City* (Manchester: Manchester University Press, 2000). Chapter 8, pp. 193-222. '"Birmingham's What I Think With": Roy Fisher's Cities'. See especially 'Fisher's Composite Urban Epic', pp. 196-202. This is a revised version of '"Birmingham's What I Think With": Roy Fisher's Composite Epic', *Yale Journal of Criticism*, 13:1, Spring 2000, pp.87-106.

Robert Sheppard, *The Poetry of Saying: British Poetry and its Discontents* (Liverpool: University of Liverpool Press, 2005). Chapter Three: 'Starting to Make a World: The Poetry of Roy Fisher.' Other references to RF *passim*. See especially pp. 78-81 for commentary on *City*.

Bassal Almasalmah, *Transcending Boundaries: Modern*

Poetic Responses to the City. Ph.D. thesis. University of Leicester, October 2007. Chapter 2: 'Non-Metropolitan Perspectives: The City in William Carlos Williams and Roy Fisher'. Available at: https://core.ac.uk/display/42015672/tab/similar-list.

Robert Sheppard, 'Editorial: *City* at Fifty', *Journal of British and Irish Innovative Poetry*, 3:1, March 2011, pp. 5-8.

Andrew Crozier, 'Signs of Identity: Roy Fisher's *A Furnace*', *An Andrew Crozier Reader*, ed. Ian Brinton (Manchester: Carcanet, 2012), pp. 209-29. References to *City passim*. This essay by Andrew Crozier had previously appeared in *PN Review*, 83, 8:3, January/February 1992.

Louise Chamberlain, '*Birmingham is What I Think With*': *Urban Environments in the Poetry of Roy Fisher*. Paper presented at the PGR Symposium, University of Nottingham, May 2013.

Gael Turnbull, *More Words: Gael Turnbull on Poets and Poetry*, ed. Jill Turnbull and Hamish Whyte (Bristol: Shearsman Books, 2012). Section IV, 'British Poets', contains 'Resonances & Speculations, upon reading Roy Fisher's *City*', pp. 142ff, and 'Some Notes on *The Ship's Orchestra*', pp. 149ff.

Linda Marshall, 'Some Modernist Poetic Myths – Part Three', *All Poetry* (blog), n.d. *c*. 2013. Brief commentary on *City* in relation to William Carlos Williams' *Paterson*. Available at: https://allpoetry.com/column/10848379-Some-modernist-poetic-myths---Part-Three-by-Linda-Marshall.

David R. Miller, *The Problem of the City: Urban Anxieties in Twentieth Century British and American Poetics*. Ph.D. thesis, Manchester Metropolitan University, 2013. Ch. 3

includes a discussion of RF's poetry. Available at: https: //e-space.mmu.ac.uk/332144/1/Final%20Thesis%20(1). pdf.

Peter Robinson, 'Conflicts in Form: The Politics of Roy Fisher's *City*', *Contemporary Political Poetry in Britain and Ireland.* Anglistik & Englischunterricht Series. ed. Uve Klawitter and Claus-Ulrich Viol (Heidelberg: Universitatsverlag Winter, 2013), pp. 95-116.

Ameeth Varma Vijay, *Misplaced Communities: The Reproduction of Materiality in Twentieth Century Planning and British Literature.* Ph.D. dissertation, University of California, 2015. Ch.2, 'The Concrete Futurity of the Postwar: Materiality in Ian Hamilton and Roy Fisher'. Available at: https://escholarship.org/content/qt9f49r7pg/ qt9f49r7pg.pdf?nosplash=e8b05d45e26c43b664453613f4 648cc9